Algarve

DIRECTIONS

WRITTEN AND RESEARCHED BY

Matthew Hancock

WITH ADDITIONAL ACCOUNTS BY

Amanda Tomlin

ROUGH
GUIDES

NEW YORK • LONDON • DELHI

www.roughguides.com

Contents

Introduction to

The Algarve

▼ Tavira

With some of Europe's best sandy beaches, idyllic rocky coves, fresh seafood and picturesque fishing villages, the Algarve is justifiably the most popular region in Portugal for both overseas visitors and the Portuguese themselves. It's a year-round destination, with bright, mild winters and long, balmy summers; it's rare for the sun not to make an appearance even in midwinter, and a local Algarve saying maintains that "Saturday without sun is like Sunday without a church service".

At just 240km from east to west and 40km from north to south at its widest point, it is easy to take in the region's big sights in a relatively short space of time. There is a good network of roads, an efficient bus service and quaint railway line, making all places relatively accessible from the airport at Faro, the regional capital.

Popularity has led to heavy development on the central coastal strip from Faro west to Lagos. But even here you can find quiet cove

▼ Alvor

beaches and vestiges of traditional Portugal amongst the panoply of villas, hotels and sports complexes. It is this combination of natural beauty and superb facilities that has made the region popular with celebrities and sports stars, from Cliff Richard and Madonna to a fair proportion of the England football team.

Development is much less pronounced at the two extremes of the Algarve. Around Sagres and along the west coast, low-key resorts are close to a series of breathtaking, wave-battered beaches, popular with surfers. To the east, relaxed resorts lie within reach of island sandbanks boasting giant swathes of dune-backed beaches. Away from the coast, inland Algarve has a surprisingly diverse landscape, with lush orange groves and wooded mountains offering superb walking territory around Monchique and Silves to the west and the Serra do Caldeirão in the centre. In the east, a more wildly beautiful landscape marks the border with Spain along the fertile Guadiana river valley.

▲ Praia de São Rafael

When to visit

Sunny, warm weather with barely a cloud in sight is pretty much guaranteed in high season (late May to early October); during this time most resorts are bustling. Peak season is in July and August, with temperatures of 25–30°C, though cooling Atlantic breezes usually make things comfortable.

Golfers ensure that autumn remains a busy season, as the cooler breezes off the coast in September and October are ideal for the game. But it is not too cool for beachgoers either, and swimming is tempting well into October (and year-round if you're hardy, with water temperatures rarely dropping below 15°C).

The region is perhaps at its best in spring or winter, with temperatures usually a pleasant 15–18°C, the countryside at its most lush and the resorts delightfully quiet. Despite the chance of the occasional downpour, most hotels and restaurants stay open, and many hotels offer generous discounts.

The Algarve

AT A GLANCE

WEST OF FARO

The international airport is at the regional capital Faro, a picturesque and historic harbour town. Within easy reach are the purpose-built resorts of Quinta do Lago, Vale de Lobo and Vilamoura, each with grand beaches, international restaurants and a brace of golf courses and sports facilities which has led the area to be dubbed "Sportugal".

THE EASTERN ALGARVE

Characterful towns such as Olhão, Fuzeta and Tavira are just a short ride from some of the region's most spectacular beaches – although much of the eastern Algarve is fronted by the Parque Natural da Ria Formosa, important wetlands protected by a series of six barrier islands.

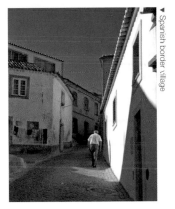

▲ Spanish border village

▲ Tavira

THE SPANISH BORDER

The historic border town of Vila Real de Santo António gives easy access to Spain and sits on the verdant Guadiana river. This natural boundary with Spain is bolstered by impressive fortresses in the villages of Alcoutim and Castro Marim. West of here lies a wild mountainous landscape of small agricultural villages and spectacular scenery.

THE CENTRAL ALGARVE

The central stretch of coast contains the classic postcard images of the province – tiny bays, broken up by rocky outcrops and

ish capital Silves, en route to the Serra de Monchique, the highest mountain range in the south, with great walks through the cork and chestnut woods, and a beautiful old spa village in Caldas de Monchique.

THE SOUTHWEST ALGARVE

The southwest Algarve embraces Lagos, one of the region's liveliest historic towns with some great beaches; and continues up to the cape at Sagres – once site of Henry the Navigator's naval school and the most southwesterly point of mainland Europe. In between, development is restricted around the former fishing villages of Luz, Burgau and Salema, each with fine, cliff-backed beaches.

fantastic grottoes, at their most exotic around the major resorts of Albufeira, Armação de Pêra and Carvoeiro. Here you'll find some of the region's biggest – if most developed – beaches at Galé, Praia da Rocha and Alvor.

THE WEST COAST

Part of the Parque Natural do Sudoeste Alentejano e Costa Vicentina, the protected west coast shows a very different face of the Algarve. Cooler waters and crashing surf lie off the majestic beaches near Vila do Bispo, Carrapateira, Aljezur and Odeceixe. The area is thin on accommodation but very popular with surfers and those into unspoilt terrain.

INLAND

The inland Algarve is remarkably unspoilt, with picture-postcard villages such as Alte and Salir a world away from the coastal resorts. Here you'll find the Moor-

Ideas

The big six

Rightly famed for its stupendous beaches and year-round sunshine, the Algarve also boasts a diverse range of attractions from whitewashed former fishing villages to ancient walled towns, and from wild mountain scenery to atmospheric wetlands. There's enough to keep visitors busy for weeks, though as the region is relatively small, you can see many of the following sights in just a few days.

▲ Lagos

This attractive, historic walled town sits within walking distance of pristine beaches and a sculpted coastline where boats can take you to visit rock pillars, blowholes and amazing grottoes.

P.151 ▸ LAGOS AND AROUND

▲ Albufeira

The region's most popular resort has a bit of everything: a superb town beach, a dazzling whitewashed old town, various watersports and a nightlife where just about anything goes.

P.107 ▸ ALBUFEIRA AND AROUND

▲ Silves

Surrounded by orange groves, the former Moorish capital looks much as it has done for centuries, with a superb castle and historic cathedral.

▼ Serra de Monchique

Alluring footpaths and mountain roads crisscross the beautiful wooded hills around Monchique, offering a peaceful alternative to the bustling beach resorts

▲ Parque Natural da Costa Vicentina

The protected west coast of the Algarve is a surfers' paradise, a largely undiscovered stretch of wild coastline studded with exhilarating wave-battered beaches.

▼ Reserva Natural da Ria Formosa

Six unique barrier islands protecting a system of salt marshes and tidal mudflats, each fronted by sandspit beaches that spread as far as the eye can see.

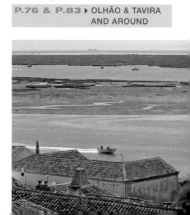

Beaches

Few places in Europe have so many Blue Flag beaches in such a concentrated area. The east has enormous stretches of sand, many on offshore islets that can be reached by boat. The central region has more accessible sands, some sheltered by low cliffs. The west coast beaches tend to be broad sandy bays facing thunderous breakers. All face the Atlantic – though never as warm as the Med, it's never as cold out of season, and hardy swimmers take to the water all year.

▲ Ilha de Tavira

The most popular sandspit beach, with some fourteen kilometres of soft sands that attract families and a young crowd.

P.85 ▶ TAVIRA AND AROUND

▲ Praia da Marinha

Topped by a delightful coastal path, this is one of the least visited of the cliff-backed coves in the central Algarve.

P.120 ▶ ARMAÇÃO DE PERA AND AROUND

▲ Sagres

Plenty of soft sands offering water sports are to be found around the western town of Sagres.

P.169 ▶ SAGRES AND AROUND

▶ Praia de Dona Ana

Perhaps the most photographed of the Algarve's beaches, this distinctive cove with its rock pillars and caves is best visited out of season.

P.155 ▶ LAGOS AND AROUND

▼ Praia de São Rafael

This highly picturesque cove beach is studded with sandstone pillars.

P.111 ▶ ALBUFEIRA AND AROUND

▲ Praia da Falésia

Backed by distinctive reddish cliffs, this long stretch of beach is overlooked by some of the most exclusive of the Algarve's hotels.

P.65 ▶ WEST OF FARO

Historical Algarve

The Romans inevitably left their mark on the Algarve. However, it was the Moors – who occupied the region for around five hundred years until 1249 – who most influenced the architecture, farming, *azulejos* (tiles) and place names of the region (whose name comes from the Arabic *al-Gharb*, "the west"). In the fifteenth century, the Algarve's ports became the main departure points for the great Portuguese navigators; even today, their legacy can be seen in many of the region's churches and monuments.

▲ Milreu

The area's most important Roman site, complete with fish mosaics, a bath house and the remains of one of the earliest Christian churches in the world.

P.73 ▶ NORTH OF FARO

▲ Lagos

The country's first slave market appeared in Lagos in 1444. The trade ironically helped finance further maritime explorations and by the mid-sixteenth century, Portugal – along with Spain – dominated world trade, with trading posts from Macau in the east to Brazil in the west.

P.153 ▶ LAGOS AND AROUND

▶ Sagres

The instigator of the great maritime explorations, Henry the Navigator set up a School of Navigation at this windswept promontory in around 1420, opening up the unknown world to Portugal's traders.

P.169 ▶ SAGRES AND AROUND

▼ Vila Real

The Great Earthquake of 1755 did much to end Portugal's glory days, but Vila Real became a symbol of post-quake Portugal. Its grid of streets were built using the same town planning techniques as had been used in Lisbon.

P.98 ▶ VILA REAL, THE GUADIANA AND THE SERRA DE ALCARIA

▲ Silves

Silves was one of Iberia's most important Moorish centres until 1189, when it was captured by Christians under Dom Sancho I, whose statue still guards the walls.

P.130 ▶ SILVES AND AROUND

▶ Vilamoura

Low-density, high-tech and stuffed with sports amenities, Vilamoura represents the future of the Algarve, a purpose-built resort catering to the tastes of the Euro zone.

P.63 ▶ WEST OF FARO

Best museums

Though none of the Algarve's museums can be described as unmissable, they do offer an insight into the culture, crafts and traditions that make the Algarve so proud of its distinct identity. Many of the museums are set in buildings that are worth a visit in their own right, and entry fees rarely exceed €3. As elsewhere in Portugal, most museums close on Mondays.

▲ Museu Arqueologia, Silves

Partly set in the old town walls, Silves' archaeological museum romps through Portugal's history with a diverse range of exhibits, including an intact 10m-deep Moorish well.

P.132 ▸ SILVES AND AROUND

▲ Museu Arqueológico, Loulé

Set within Loulé's castle, this tiny museum shows off the foundations of a Moorish house, re-creates a traditional kitchen and allows visitors access to the castle walls.

P.70 ▸ NORTH OF FARO

▲ Museu Etnográfico do Trajo Algarvio, São Bras de Alportel

Neatly preserved agricultural equipment, a traditional well and historical costumes add up to one of the most engaging of the Algarve's cultural museums.

P.72 ▸ NORTH OF FARO

▲ Museu Arqueológico, Faro

Housed in an ancient convent with one of the most beautiful cloisters in the country, Faro's main museum also displays Moorish lamps, Roman mosaics and some fine modern paintings.

P.53 ▸ FARO AND AROUND

▶ Museu Regional, Lagos

An eclectic, treasure trove-cum-junk shop of a museum, with everything from Roman busts to crafts and rusting surgical instruments.

P.154 ▸ LAGOS AND AROUND

Castles

The Algarve has historically been vulnerable to attack, and fortifications became essential to protect the key settlements. Many of today's castles are adaptations of originally Moorish structures; others were built in the thirteenth century during the reign of Dom Dinis, one of the country's first monarchs who saw the importance of strengthening his frontiers. Today, some castles function as museums, but most are tranquil hilltop retreats from which to admire the local views.

▲ Paderne

Apart from the nearby highway, Paderne's ruined Moorish castle sits in splendid rural isolation.

P.112 ▶ ALBUFEIRA AND AROUND

▲ Silves

Though the interior is undergoing restoration, the exterior dominates the town and is one of the most impressive fortifications in the region.

P.130 ▶ SILVES AND AROUND

▲ Ferragudo

Though not open to the public, Ferragudo's sixteenth-century Castelo de São João do Arade is one of the only castles in the region impressively sited right on the beach itself.

P.127 ▸ CARVOEIRO AND AROUND

▼ Aljezur

The remains of the tenth-century Moorish castle quietly brood on a hilltop overlooking this pretty town in the western Algarve.

P.177 ▸ THE WEST COAST

▲ Castro Marim

Facing the Spanish border, this thirteenth-century stronghold was the former head-quarters of the Order of Christ, a chivalric order who protected Portugal's remote areas for the Church and king.

P.101 ▸ VILA REAL, THE GUADIANA AND THE SERRA DE ALCARIA

Churches

Though the religious centre of Portugal is in Braga, in the north, the Catholic Church has been highly influential to the Algarve's development. Many churches date from the Golden Age of the sixteenth century, when funds were lavished on ornate, maritime-influenced carvings and Gothic-influenced architecture known as the Manueline style. Many of the churches withstood the devastating earthquake of 1755 and today remain some of the region's oldest and most rewarding places to visit, rich in architecture and *azulejos*.

▲ Igreja de Santo António, Lagos

This fantastically embellished, barrel-vaulted, eighteenth-century church is a masterpiece of Baroque architecture.

P.154 ▶ LAGOS AND AROUND

▲ Nossa Senhora de Guadalupe

Local tradition maintains that Henry the Navigator was a frequent visitor to this thirteenth-century church set in a lonely field.

P.164 ▶ THE SOUTH WEST COAST

▲ Nossa Senhora de Piedade, Loulé

One of the most distinctive of the region's modern churches, which also plays centre stage to the important Mãe Soberana Easter parade.

▼ Sé Velha, Faro

Faro's cathedral is the most important church in the Algarve, much of it dating from the thirteenth century.

▲ Igreja Matriz, Alvor

A sixteenth-century church embellished with the distinctive Manueline architectural style, all twisted pillars and ornate carved doors.

On the tiles

Decorative tiles – *azulejos* – can be seen both inside and outside houses, churches, cafés and even train stations. The craft was brought to Iberia by the Moors in the eighth century; the word derives from the Arabic *al-zulecha*, "small stone". Changing technology and fashions have led to various styles of *azulejo* panels, including religious imagery, decorative tiled walls known as *tapetes* (rugs), Rococo designs, satirical portraits and contemporary designs.

▲ Igreja de São Laurenço, Almancil

The church's interior is lined with sumptuous tiles depicting the life of Saint Lawrence, painted in 1730 by one of the country's leading artists.

P.60 ▶ WEST OF FARO

▲ Market, Quarteira

Tiles also illustrate the contents of shops and markets, as here outside Quarteira market.

P.62 ▶ WEST OF FARO

▼ Flats, Monte Gordo

Useful both for insulation and decoration, tiles are still used on buildings to this day.

P.94 ▶ THE EASTERN ALGARVE

▲ Backstreets, Olhão

Ornate *azulejos* decorate some of the humblest houses, like these ones in Olhão.

P.76 ▶ OLHÃO AND AROUND

▼ Hotel Bela Vista, Praia da Rocha

This beautiful, early twentieth-century hotel displays the best in Portuguese interior decor.

P.140 ▶ PORTIMÃO, PRAIA DA ROCHA AND AROUND

Nature

The Algarve's wildlife varies from wild boar in the interior to rare wading birds on the coastal mudflats. Plant life is also abundant: carob, citrus and olive trees were introduced by the Moors, and some olive trees are believed to be up to one thousand years old. Almond trees contribute to many of the region's marzipan-based sweets, and blossom spectacularly in February, earning them the nickname "snow of the Algarve". Another welcome species is the umbrella pine, which offers shade to many golf courses.

▲ São Bras de Alportel

Some fifty percent of the world's cork supplies come from southern Portugal, and the ancient cork groves around São Bras offer a habitat for wild boar, foxes and the extremely rare Iberian lynx.

P.72 ▶ NORTH OF FARO

▲ Parque Natural da Ria Formosa

One of the most important wetlands in Iberia, sheltering various fish, reptiles and wading birds; the reserve's rarest species is the purple galinule, a stumpy, swamp-loving bird.

P.61 ▶ WEST OF FARO

▲ Quinta da Rocha

This flat river estuary supports some 22 species of wading bird, such as the sanderling and knot.

P.140 ▶ PORTIMÃO, PRAIA DA ROCHA AND AROUND

▼ Reserva Natural do Sapal de Castro Marim

The marshy riverside reserve near the Spanish border is home to spoonbills, winter flamingos and the rare swivel-eyed Mediterranean chameleon, famed for its phenomenally long tongue.

P.101 ▶ VILA REAL, THE GUADIANA AND THE SERRA DE ALCARIA

▲ Cabo de São Vicente

Portugal's most southwesterly point supports the highest proportion of marine and bird life in the country, including sea otters, Bonelli's eagles, ospreys, kites and white herons, especially in spring and autumn.

P.172 ▶ SAGRES AND AROUND

Sport

The Algarve has some of Europe's best year-round sports facilities. Famed for its golf (see p.28), the region also has world-class tennis centres and well-equipped marinas. With its swell sizes of up to fifteen feet, Portugal is one of Europe's top surfing destinations, while windsurfing and kite surfing are also growing in popularity. You can see top soccer action at the futuristic Faro-Loulé stadium, and – though not something all tourists wish to support – bullfights take place in Albufeira.

▲ Kite surfing

The west coast offers ideal conditions for a high-adrenaline sport in which a giant kite whisks you across the waves.

P.171 ▶ SAGRES AND AROUND

ALBUFEIRA
A CORRIDA DOS TRIUNFADORES
BULLFIGHT
AGOSTO/AUGUST-2004
QUINTA 19
THURSDAY
22.00 H - 10.00 P.M. - U.M. 22.00
6 IMPONENTES TOIROS 6
Ganadaria 1981 Sesmarias Velhas Guadiana Ferro F.S.
JOÃO
CAVALEIROS
MOURA
ANTÓNIO RIBEIRO
TELLES

▲ Bullfights

During the summer, bullfights take place twice weekly at Albufeira's Praça dos Touros; tickets cost around €25.

P.111 ▶ ALBUFEIRA AND AROUND

▲ Soccer

Part of the Parque das Cidades sports park, the futuristic thirty-thousand all-seater Faro-Loulé stadium was purpose-built for Euro 2004, a great venue for international or local league matches.

P.55 ▶ FARO AND AROUND

▼ Windsurfing

With constant winds averaging force 3–5, the Algarve offers excellent windsurfing, with many windsurfing schools like this one at Praia da Martinhal.

P.171 ▶ SAGRES AND AROUND

▲ Tennis

The Vale de Lobo Tennis Academy, run by ex-Portuguese pro Pedro Frazão, is frequented by Tim Henman and is the highest rated of the region's many tennis centres.

P.62 ▶ WEST OF FARO

◀ Surfing

The west coast beach of Arrifana offers fine surf for beginners, while pros also visit for the occasional competitions. For details, check ⓦwww.surfing-waves.com.

P.178 ▶ THE WEST COAST

Top golf courses

Portugal's year-round mild climate and top facilities make it ideal for golf. Not surprisingly, the Algarve's courses are not cheap, with green fees at up to €150 for eighteen holes. The best way to guarantee a round is to go on a special golf-holiday package (try @www.playgolfinportugal.com) or to stay at one of the hotels or villas attached to golf clubs, which usually charge guests discounted rates (of up to fifty percent). For more information, see the excellent @www.algarvegolf.net.

▲ Alto Golf

Try your luck at one of Europe's longest holes, at 604 metres, at the Henry Cotton-designed Alto Golf Club near Alvor.

P.191 ▶ ESSENTIALS

▲ Pine Cliffs

Designed by Martin Hawtree, the highly picturesque Pine Cliffs is famed for its par three sixth hole across a rocky gorge, perhaps the most photographed golf shot in Europe.

P.191 ▶ ESSENTIALS

▼ Penina

With some wicked bunkers, this is rated one of the hardest courses in the region and has held the Portuguese Open eight times.

P.191 ▸ ESSENTIALS

▲ Quinta do Lago

Rated one of Europe's top golf complexes, and frequently venue for the Portuguese Open, this has eighteen holes designed by William Mitchell.

P.191 ▸ ESSENTIALS

▼ Royal Golf Course, Vale de Lobo

Rocky Roquemore's eighteen-hole Royal Golf Course incorporates two impressive bunkers in the form of ravines plunging into the beach.

P.191 ▸ ESSENTIALS

▲ The Old Course, Vilamoura

Originally designed by Frank Pennink and refurbished in 1996 by Martin Hawtree, The Old Course is known for its daunting bunkers and water features, much of it under shady umbrella pines.

P.191 ▸ ESSENTIALS

Kids' Algarve

With top hotels, a range of villas and miles of beach, the Algarve is perfect for family holidays. The Portuguese are very family-orientated and children are welcomed everywhere – expect to see children out in public squares and restaurants until midnight. There are also various attractions specially for children, including water parks, zoos and mini-train rides. Coin-operated rides also feature outside shops and cafés, while playgrounds are to be found all over the region.

▲ Zoo Marine

Part zoo, part theme park and wholly delightful for kids, with performing dolphins, sea lions, birds and various aquatic beasties.

P.114 ▶ ALBUFEIRA AND AROUND

▲ Pedras d'el Rei

Getting to the superb beach at Barril is half the fun, on the toy train from the holiday village of Pedras d'El Rei.

P.87 ▶ TAVIRA AND AROUND

▶ The Big One

Around 1.5 km of water chutes – plus a giant frog – await at the Big One, the Algarve's largest water park.

P.120 ▶ ARMAÇÃO DE PÊRA AND AROUND

▼ Lagos Zoo

Wallabies, monkeys, Vietnamese pigs and exotic birds roam this well laid-out zoo northwest of Lagos.

P.157 ▶ LAGOS AND AROUND

◀ Krazy World

Another zoo-cum-theme park boasting fairground rides, animal parks, crazy golf and quad bikes.

P.112 ▶ ALBUFEIRA AND AROUND

▼ Slide and Splash

The name says it all, as does the Kamikaze, one of several high-thrill water slides and chutes.

P.125 ▶ CARVOEIRO AND AROUND

Shops and markets

Amongst the tourist souvenirs, you can still find traditional arts and crafts in the region's shops and markets. Distinctive ceramics, copperwork, hand-knitted chunky jumpers and wooden furniture are of good quality and usually good value. So, too, are local food and drink specialities, such as cheeses and almond-based sweets and wines. These can be best value at covered markets, to be found in all the main towns. Many towns also have a weekly gypsy market, superb places for atmosphere and the odd bargain garment. For shopping hours see p.193.

▲ Chic shopping, Faro

Its pedestrianized shopping streets offer the best in Portuguese chic, while the giant Fórum Algarve shopping centre contains some two hundred shops.

P.56 ▸ FARO AND AROUND

▲ Markets, Loulé

Visit on a Saturday morning, when the covered market is at its most animated and the gypsy market visits the edges of town.

▼ Folding chairs, Monchique

These beautifully crafted and distinctive scissor chairs are typical of the region and make fine souvenirs.

▼ Ceramics workshops, Porches

Porches is famed for its distinctive majolica pottery, but you can also buy ceramics from all over Portugal.

Boat trips

One of the best ways to appreciate the Algarve's dramatic coastal scenery is to take a boat trip. These range from hour-long cruises to full- or half-day excursions, often including a picnic lunch. Specialist fishing or dolphin-watching trips are also available. You can also explore inland, either on the waterways of the eastern Algarve or up the rivers Arade and Guadiana. The latter divides Portugal from Spain, and a fun excursion is to take a boat trip into the neighbouring country.

▲ Lagos

Some of the region's most dramatic rock formations can be seen by boat off Ponta da Piedade, the headland jutting out beyond Lagos.

P.153 ▸ LAGOS AND AROUND

▲ Vila Real to Spain

The ferry to Spain is a delightful trip across the Guadiana to the picturesque border town of Ayamonte.

P.100 ▸ VILA REAL, THE GUADIANA AND THE SERRA DE ALCARIA

▶ Parque Natural da Ria Formosa

Safari boat trips like this one from Santa Luzia explore the important wetlands and beaches of the Parque Natural da Ria Formosa.

P.86 ▶ TAVIRA AND AROUND

▼ Up the Guadiana

Regular trips run from the border town of Vila Real pass up the Guadiana, with Spain on one side and Portugal on the other, through idyllic, unspoilt countryside.

P.102 ▶ VILA REAL, THE GUADIANA AND THE SERRA DE ALCARIA

▲ Vilamoura

The marina offers countless boat trips – head up the coast past Cliff Richard's villa, and if you are lucky dolphins will follow in your wake.

P.64 ▶ WEST OF FARO

Prettiest villages

Decades of tourism have left their mark on the region, and many of the former tranquil fishing villages are all but lost in a tangle of villa complexes. But there are still some settlements that have remained unscathed and highly picturesque, from atmospheric fishing villages to dazzling whitewashed mountain hamlets. Even these places get summer visitors, but go out of season or at the end of the day and they reveal what the Algarve was like a century ago.

▲ Alte

Often billed as the prettiest village in the Algarve, its dazzling white houses are lit up by geraniums close to tranquil natural springs.

P.113 ▸ ALBUFEIRA AND AROUND

▲ Cacela Velha

This little clifftop town looks much as it must have for centuries, overlooking its distant sandspit beach.

P.93 ▸ THE EASTERN ALGARVE

▲ Alcoutim

A picture-book border village with its own castle facing the river Guadiana, and a mirror-image village over the border in Spain.

P.103 ▸ VILA REAL, THE GUADIANA AND THE SERRA DE ALCARIA

▼ Salir

A traditional inland village boasting the remains of a Moorish castle in the heart of rolling countryside.

P.71 ▸ NORTH OF FARO

▶ Caldas de Monchique

Avoid the midday coach parties and this tiny spa village is delightfully tranquil, set in the heart of chestnut woods in the Serra de Monchique.

P.145 ▸ SERRA DE MONCHIQUE

Festivals and events

Though superficially less exuberant than their Spanish neighbours, the Portuguese certainly know how to have a good time when it comes to festivals, and virtually every village in the Algarve has at least one of these at some stage of the year. Most of these revolve round celebrating the patron saint of the community with a few pagan traditions thrown in for good measure. A church service is usually followed by a parade, music and dancing, with plenty of alcohol.

▲ Almond blossom, Guadiana

The spectacular blossoming of the almond trees in January and February is known as the snow of the Algarve – legend has it after a Moorish king planted the trees to placate his Swedish wife who pined for the snows of winter.

P.102 ▸ VILA REAL, THE GUADIANA AND THE SERRA DE ALCARIA

▲ Festa de Santos Populares, Tavira

June sees riotous street parties celebrating the popular saints of António (12–13), João (23–24) and Pedro (28–29); Tavira's Festa de Santo António is one of the liveliest.

P.190 ▸ ESSENTIALS

▶ Sardine festival, Quarteira

Row upon row of sizzling bodies may be nothing new on Quarteira's beaches, but in August grilled sardines take centre stage, with a massive set-up on the beach.

P.62 ▶ WEST OF FARO

▼ Beer Festival, Silves

Silves suddenly becomes a very popular destination when international and local beers are quaffed by the barrel, usually in July.

P.132 ▶ SILVES AND AROUND

▲ Mãe Soberana, Loulé

The region's most important religious festival, when an image of Our Lady of Piety is carried into town in an Easter procession.

P.71 ▶ NORTH OF FARO

◀ Carnival, Loulé

Loulé's carnival parade is one of the most colourful in the region.

P.69 ▶ NORTH OF FARO

Food and drink

A plate of fresh sardines with a cool beer at sunset is one of the quintessential Portuguese beachside experiences, but there is more to the local cuisine than that. Much of Portugal's fantastic seafood comes from the Algarve, and you shouldn't miss the opportunity to sample its prawns, clams or unique seafood dishes. Fresh fish is generally affordable, varied and nearly always excellent, grilled meats are reliably tasty, while a decent local wine can be enjoyed at even the humblest of cafés.

▲ Pastéis de Nata

The recipe for these custard tartlets has been Portugal's most successful export since Ronaldo. They are best enjoyed sprinkled with cinnamon and washed down with a coffee outside a café like *Gardy* in Faro.

P.57 ▶ FARO AND AROUND

▲ Presunto

Presunto – smoked ham – is one of the little-known delights of southern Portugal, and some of the best come from the mountains round Monchique. It even has its own ham festival in July.

P.146 ▶ SERRA DE MONCHIQUE

▲ Wine

Inexpensive and drinkable, most of the Algarve's wines come from Lagoa, though wines from Estremadura, Ribatejo and the Douro are even better.

P.160 ▶ LAGOS AND AROUND

▼ Sardines

The traditional Portuguese dish, *sardinhas no churrasco* (grilled sardines) are said to be best when there is no "r" in the month (ie May–Aug). Olhão market shows how fresh they can be.

P.76 ▶ OLHÃO AND AROUND

▲ Cataplana

The delicious fish bouillabaisse-type dish takes its name from the copper pans that they are cooked in, a vessel dating back to Moorish times. *O Patio* in Tavira specializes in various types.

P.90 ▶ TAVIRA AND AROUND

Cafés, bars and clubs

Portugal has a thriving café society and it is easy to fall into the local custom of punctuating the day with regular drink stops. Every town and resort has a fine range of café-bars, from Art Deco wonders with marble tabletops to flash steel-and-chrome designer buildings serving the latest cocktails. Most of the big resorts have at least one glitzy club too; most get going at around midnight and keep going until the small hours.

▲ Rua Candido dos Reis, Albufeira

This narrow pedestrianized strip is lined with bars vying to outdo each other with the loudest music and rudest-named cocktail.

P.108 ▶ ALBUFEIRA AND AROUND

▲ Café Calcina, Loulé

Tuck into a beer and *tremoços* (pickled lupin seeds) at Loulé's most atmospheric café.

P.75 ▶ NORTH OF FARO

▲ Café Inglês, Silves

Arty converted town house nestling on cobbled steps below Silves castle, with frequent exhibitions along with fine food and drink.

P.134 ▶ SILVES AND AROUND

▼ Anazu, Tavira

The perfect suntrap for a breakfast or evening drink, facing the Rio Gilão.

P.89 ▶ TAVIRA AND AROUND

▲ Sete, Vilamoura

Part-owned by Luís Figo, this bar overlooking Vilamoura marina is perfect for star-spotting by day or night.

P.68 ▶ WEST OF FARO

Restaurants

Eating out at a restaurant is a popular pastime for most Portuguese, so restaurants are plentiful and inexpensive. Upmarket restaurants often grab the top locations, but you can still find affordable places right on the beachfronts. The atmospheric backstreets are where you'll often find the liveliest local haunts, often with a TV in one corner, children running round until midnight, and filling food.

▲ A Ruina, Albufeira

Partly set in the ruins of the old town walls, tables are set out on the sands in summer for superbly grilled fish.

P.117 ▶ ALBUFEIRA AND AROUND

▲ A Tasca

Enjoy fish and seafood straight from the harbour below in this atmospheric clifftop restaurant.

P.174 ▶ SAGRES AND AROUND

▲ Rei das Praias, Praia de Caneiros

Top food in a great location, in a simple beach restaurant on the beach, makes a meal here a memorable occasion.

P.128 ▸ CARVOEIRO AND AROUND

▼ Caminé

Politicians and stars like to dine at this swish restaurant offering deluxe Portuguese cuisine facing a lagoon.

P.57 ▸ FARO AND AROUND

▲ Dona Barca, Portimão

One of the region's most highly rated restaurants, with outside seats on a tranquil patio.

P.142 ▸ PORTIMÃO, PRAIA DA ROCHA AND AROUND

Weird and wonderful

Some of the Algarve's charm lies in the unexpected sights that you come across when exploring the region – from ragged storks' nests that cap the chimneys and church towers in early summer to remote hamlets where women still wear traditional dress, and from farmers tilling their fields with mules to schools of dolphins suddenly rising out of the waves.

▲ Aquatic poodles, Quinta da Marim

It may sound like a shaggy dog story, but these aquatic dogs really were bred to help chase fish into fishermen's nets.

P.78 ▸ OLHÃO AND AROUND

▲ Rosa dos Ventos, Sagres

This extraordinary wind compass, used to measure the wind direction, may date back to the time of Henry the Navigator.

P.170 ▸ SAGRES AND AROUND

▼ Door knockers, Tavira

Ornate hands are poised over Tavira's doors as they have been for centuries.

P.83 ▸ TAVIRA AND AROUND

▲ The lighthouse, Cabo de São Vicente

Marking what was once considered the edge of the world, this lighthouse has the most powerful beam in Europe.

P.172 ▸ SAGRES AND AROUND

▼ Capela dos Ossos, Faro

One way to line your walls – this bizarre chapel is completely decorated with human bones.

P.54 ▸ FARO AND AROUND

Places

Faro and around

With its international airport, impressive shopping centre and ring of high-rise apartments, Faro boasts something of a big city feel. The central area, however, is both attractive and manageable, and its harbourside gardens, semi-walled old town and range of shops make it a fine place to start or finish a tour of the region. It has been the administrative capital of the Algarve since 1776. The Romans, Moors and Spanish all ruled for a time, though today's mosaic-paved pedestrianized streets around Rua de Santo António are decidedly Portuguese in character, filled with aromatic cafés, restaurants and shops. Faro is cut off from the sea by a marshy lagoon, but lies within easy reach of two fine sandspit beaches as well as the impressive Faro-Loulé stadium.

The harbour

The *doca* (harbour) is Faro's natural focus: the town gardens and a cluster of outdoor cafés overlook the rows of sleek yachts and at the end of the day, much of Faro gathers to promenade here. To the north there's a small **Museu Marítimo** (℡289 894 990; Mon–Fri 2.30 4.30pm; free), a modest maritime museum with engaging displays of model boats and local fishing techniques.

On the other side of the harbour, you can follow the railway line for an attractive walk along the seafront, with the town walls on one side and the mud flats on the other; a small arch through the old town walls offers an approach to the Cidade Velha (see overleaf).

From the jetty opposite here, ferries depart to the local sandspit beaches (see p.55).

▼FARO MARINA

Faro and around PLACES

Centro Ciência Viva

Rua Comandante Francisco Manuel ☎289 890 920. July to mid-Sept Tues–Sun 4–11pm; mid-Sept to June Tues–Fri 10am–5pm, Sat & Sun 3–7pm. €2.50, under 12s €1. The Centro Ciência Viva (Centre for Living Science) is a good wet-weather spot, especially for kids. Set in the town's former elec-tricity-generating station, with an attractive roof terrace at the back, there are several low-tech interactive exhibits that explain scientific principles. Exhibits change but the most popular permanent attraction is a flight simulator. Most of the displays are labelled only in Portuguese.

Cidade Velha

The oldest and most picturesque part of Faro, the Cidade Velha (old town) is an oval of cobbled streets and whitewashed build-ings set within sturdy town walls,

parts of which you can climb for great views over the town. The most striking entrance to the old town is through the nineteenth-century town gate, the Arco da Vila, next to the turismo. The Neoclassical arch, often capped by a stork's nest, was built by the Italian architect Francisco Xavier Fabri, on a commis-sion by the Algarve's bishop, Francisco Gomes do Avelar, whose memorial sits in an alcove inside the arch. From here, Rua do Município leads up to the majestic main square, Largo da Sé, lined with orange trees and flanked by the cathedral and a group of palaces – including the former bishop's palace. The **Sé** itself (Mon–Sat 9am–12.30pm & 1.30–5pm, Sun open for Mass at 10am & noon; €1.50) is a squat, white mismatch of Gothic, Renaissance and Baroque styles, all heavily remodelled after the

▼OLD TOWN WALL, FARO

Ferries to Farol & Ilha Deserta ▼

1755 earthquake. It's worth looking inside for the fine eighteenth-century *azulejos*, though the main appeal is its clock tower, which you can climb up for superb views over the surrounding coastland.

Museu Arqueológico

Praça Afonso III ☎289 897 400. May–Sept Tues–Fri 9.30am–5.30pm, Sat & Sun 11.30am–5.30pm; Oct–April Tues–Fri 10am–6pm, Sat & Sun 2–6pm. €2. Housed in the sixteenth-century Convento de Nossa Senhora da Assunção, the Museu Arqueológico is the Algarve's oldest museum, first opened in 1894, with one of the most beautiful cloisters in the country. The most striking of the museum's exhibits is a superb fourth-century AD Roman mosaic of Neptune surrounded by the four winds, unearthed near the train station. Other

▲THE BRIDGE TO PRAIA DE FARO

items include a fine collection of Roman statues from the excavations at Estói (see p.73), exquisite Moorish lamps, vases and bowls and Baroque and Renaissance paintings from the sixteenth to nineteenth centuries. More modern are the futurist works of art by Carlos Porfírio, one of the country's leading twentieth-century painters.

Largo de São Francisco

South of the Cidade Velha and marked by an impressive fountain, the wide Largo de São Francisco serves as a giant car park for most of the year, but is cleared in late October for the Feira de Santa Iria, an enormous market-cum-fairground with live entertainment over the best part of a week. The square is overlooked by the **Igreja da Ordeu Terceira de São Francisco**, rebuilt in the eighteenth century on the site of an earlier church. Plain on the outside, the interior contains Baroque tiles and beautiful Rococo woodwork.

Igreja do Carmo and Igreja de São Pedro

Largo do Carmo ☏289 824 490. Mon–Fri 10am–1pm & 3–6pm (until 5pm Oct–April), Sat 10am–1pm, Sun only for Mass at 9am. Free, Capela

dos Ossos €1. By far the most curious sight in town lies in the twin-towered, Baroque **Igreja do Carmo**. A door to the right of the altar leads to the sacristy where you can buy a ticket for the macabre Capela dos Ossos (Chapel of Bones), set in an attractive garden. Like the one at Alcantarilha (see p.120), its walls are decorated with human bones as a reminder of human mortality – in this case disinterred in the nineteenth century from the adjacent monks' cemetery.

Nearby, on Largo de São Pedro, the sixteenth-century Igreja de São Pedro is one of the town's most attractive churches with a finely decorated altar (to the left of the main altar), whose central image is a gilded, wooden Last Supper.

Museu Regional

Praça de Liberdade 2 ☏289 827 610. Mon–Fri 9am–12.30pm & 2–5.30pm. €1.50. One of the most likeable of Faro's museums, the Museu Regional displays local crafts and industries, including reconstructions of cottage interiors and models of the net systems still used for tuna fishing. There are also black-and-white photos of the town and local beaches before tourism took hold.

Ilha Deserta and Ilha da Culatra

Ferries shuttle from Faro's jetty, just south of the Centro Ciência Viva by the town wall, through narrow marshy channels to the so-called **Ilha Deserta** (details on ☎917 811 856; June to mid-Sept 4 daily; €12 return), part of the Parque Natural da Ria Formosa and the most southerly point of mainland Portugal. The sandspit island has a superb beach, though the name is actually a misnomer, as there is a pricy café, *O Estaminé*, and plenty of other sun-worshippers for company; the island's official name is Ilha da Barreta. Alternatively there are 2.5-hour day-trips (details on ☎917 811 856; twice daily on Sun, Tues & Thurs; €20 per person, including lunch). Ferries also depart from the same jetty to Farol (see p.77) on the **Ilha da Culatra** (details on ☎917 634 813; June to mid-Sept 4 daily, first boat 9.30am, last return 7pm; €4 return).

Praia de Faro

Buses #14 and #16 from Faro's harbour gardens via the bus station and airport (daily 7.10am–9pm, 8pm at weekends, every 45 min; €1.20), terminating just before the narrow bridge to the beach. There are timetables posted at the bus stops; buy tickets on board. Lying just 3km from the airport, Praia de Faro makes a good base for a first or last night in the country. It is typical of the sandspit *ilha* beaches of the eastern Algarve: a long sweep of beautiful sand with both a sea-facing and a more sheltered lagoon-facing side. But being so near both the airport and Faro, it is inevitably overdeveloped, with bars, restaurants and villas jammed onto a sandy island almost too narrow to cope in the height of summer. Out of season, however, you'll probably have the sands to yourself. For more solitude, simply head west along the Praia de Faro towards Quinta do Lago (see p.61), where after a kilometre or so the crowds thin out.

Faro-Loulé stadium

Parque das Cidades ☎289 990 360, ⓦwww.parquecidades-eim.pt. Special bus service for international matches, concerts and events. Some 6km north of Faro, between the main Faro–Loulé road and the IP1 motorway, the futuristic Faro-Loulé sports stadium resembles an open seashell. Inaugurated in early 2004 when England took on Portugal in a friendly international, the stadium was purpose built as the main southern venue for Euro 2004. The 30,000 all-seater stadium is the centrepiece of a new cultural, sports and medical park; it's also home for Faro and Loulé's local teams, Farense and Louletano.

▼ FARO-LOULÉ STADIUM

Accommodation

Residencial Adelaide

Rua Cruz das Mestres 7–9 ☎289 802 383, ℗289 826 870. The friendly owner offers the best-value rooms in town, with spotless en-suite rooms, cable TV and an airy breakfast room. Some rooms sleep 3–4, and in summer the roof is opened for dorm beds at €10 per person. €50.

Estalagem Aeromar

Praia de Faro ☎289 817 542, ⓦwww .aeromar.net. Right by the bridge over to the sandspit, this is a good choice for anyone with an early flight the next day. Above a decent restaurant, it offers clean, comfortable rooms, some with small balconies with views either over the beach or of the planes taking off across the inner harbour. €75.

Residencial Algarve

Rua Infante Dom Henrique 52 ☎289 895 700, ⓔreservas@residencialalgarve .com. A modern *residencial* built in traditional style, this offers spruce rooms with spotless bathrooms and cable TV; breakfast is served in a little patio in summer. Good value, though the front rooms can be noisy. €80.

Hotel Eva

Avda da República 1 ☎289 001 000, ⓔeva@tdhotels.pt. This large, modern block is the town's best hotel, occupying a superb harbourfront position. Slightly worn rooms, most with balconies overlooking the old town or the marina (though the cheapest overlook the bus station). There's a restaurant, rooftop pool and a courtesy bus to the local beach. Disabled access. €136.

Residencial Pinto

Rua 1º de Maio 27 ☎ & ℗289 807 417. This welcoming if simple, budget *residencial* offers characterful rooms with marble floors, high ceilings and polished furniture. Communal bathrooms; price does not include breakfast. €35.

Residencial Samé

Rua do Bocage 66 ☎289 824 375, ℗289 804 166. A clean, modern hotel with small rooms in a block just outside the old town. Some have balconies and all come with bathrooms and TV. There's an appealing communal lounge downstairs. €75.

Pensão São Filipe

Rua Infante Dom Henrique 55 ☎ & ℗289 824 182. Run by the same owners as the *Residencial Algarve*, with similarly pristine rooms, each with cable TV and en-suite facilities. Rooms are small but high ceilinged with spinning fans, though the front ones contend with the traffic of a busy through road. €60.

Youth hostel

Rua da Policia de Segurança Pública (PSP) ☎289 826 521, ℗289 801 413. Located in a quiet spot to the north of the old town, the town's youth hostel sits next to attractive public gardens. Prices are €10 for beds in dorms of four or six people, or €24 for a double room, €29.50 en suite. You'll need a hostel card, and should book well in advance. Disabled access.

Shops

Fórum Algarve

☎289 889 300. Daily 10am–11pm. A well-designed shopping centre on the way to the airport, gathered round a fountain-filled central courtyard. Along with a multiplex cinema and various fast-food outlets, there are international stores such as Zara, Benetton, Pierre Cardin and Massimo Dutti, plus local favourites such as Sportzone and a Jumbo supermarket (closed Sun).

Rui Garrafeira

Praça Ferreira de Almeida 28 ☏289 822 803. Mon–Sat 8am–8pm. Sumptuous deli-cum-off licence selling ports and wines to suit all budgets. This is also a good place to buy some of the excellent local cheeses, as well as chocolates and confectionery.

Cafés

Café Aliança

Rua Dr. Francisco Gomes 6–11 ☏282 458 860. Daily 8am–midnight. This faded 1908 coffee house is said to be the oldest in Portugal, though the decor dates from the 1920s. Once the favoured haunt of the literary set, including Simone de Beauvoir, Fernando Pessoa and Mário Sá Carneiro, it remains wonderfully atmospheric. There are tables outside, and a full menu of inexpensive salads, omelettes, pastries and ice cream.

Gardy

Rua de Santo António 16 ☏289 824 062. Mon–Sat 8.30am–8pm. Cavernous and popular local *pastelaria* with a counter piled high with cakes and savouries. Tables spilling out onto the main pedestrianized street and a side alley make this one of the best places in town to watch the world go by.

Café Piramides

Jardim Manuel Bivar ☏289 822 964. Daily 8am–midnight. Set in a glass pavilion with a pyramid-shaped roof, this all-purpose café has tables in the attractive gardens facing the harbour; a fine place to enjoy anything from breakfast and coffee to inexpensive pizzas, ice creams and beers.

Restaurants

Adega Dois Irmãos

Largo Terreiro do Bispo 13–15 ☏289 823 337. Daily noon–11pm. Opened in 1925 by two brothers (*irmãos*) in a former welder's shop, this attractive tiled place is one of the oldest of the city's fish restaurants. The day's catch can be expensive (around €15), though the *pratos de dia* are usually better value. Despite the number of tourists passing through, service remains courteous and efficient.

Adega Nova

Rua Francisco Barreto 24 ☏289 813 433. Daily noon–11pm. This great barn of a place is an old-fashioned *adega* with Portuguese food and jugs of wine. Turn up early as the benches get packed, especially at weekends. You can eat a full meal for under €15 if you stay clear of the more pricey seafood. The adventurous can try *bife na pedra*: slices of beef that you cook at your table on a sizzling stone.

Caminé

Praia de Faro ☏289 817 539. Tues–Sun 12.30–3.30pm & 8–11pm. Just east of the former campsite and facing the inner harbour, this low glass-fronted restaurant is rated one of the Algarve's top restaurants and boasts the King of Spain and footballer Ruud Gullit as former guests. Sumptuous (and expensive) dishes include *lagosta* (lobster), *fondue de tamboril e gambas* (monkfish and prawn fondue), *cataplana* and *caldeirada*.

Faro e Benfica

Doca de Faro ☎ 289 821 422. Mon &
Wed–Sun 10.30am–2am. Closed Nov.
One of the best choices in town
for a pricey splurge on fish and
seafood, with tables facing the
town across the harbour. Specialities include *cataplanas, feijoada*
and various rice dishes.

Ginásio Clube Naval

Doca de Faro ☎ 289 823 869.
Tues–Sun noon–3pm & 7–11pm.
On a raised terrace right on
the harbour, this is one of the
few places in town where you
can dine on moderately priced
fish and grilled meats with fine
views over the mud flats. It also
has a simple downstairs café
offering inexpensive drinks with
views over the marina.

Ibn Harum/Muralhas de Faro

Rua do Repouso 1 ☎ 289 824 839.
Daily noon–3pm & 7.30–11pm.
Stylish and very pricey restaurant built into the walls of
the Cidade Velha. A series of

▼LARGO DE SÉ

Moorish-influenced rooms and
patios sprawl around a main
dining room, and there's also
a lovely outside terrace. If the
superbly cooked evening meals
of fish, seafood and meats are
beyond your means, try the
more reasonable lunchtime
menu, or just enjoy a drink or
coffee at the outdoor tables.

Mesa dos Mouros

Largo de Sé 10 ☎ 289 878 873.
Mon–Fri 12.30–3.30pm & 7.30–11pm,
Sat 7.30–11pm. Tiny, upmarket
place – so best to reserve for a
meal – serving cakes, drinks and
refined cuisine including seafood
and tasty chickpea salads. A few
outdoor tables sit on the broad
Largo de Sé itself.

Restaurante Paquete

Praia de Faro ☎ 289 817 760. May–
Sept daily 10am–10pm; Oct–April Mon,
Tues & Thurs–Sun 10am–8pm. One
of the beach's best-positioned
café-restaurants, just west of
the bridge to the beach, with a
sunny terrace facing the waves.
It offers everything from giant
toasted sandwiches and salads
to decent, full and moderately
priced Portuguese meals.

Sol e Jardim

Praça Ferreira de Almeida 22–23
☎ 289 820 030. Mon–Sat 12.30–3pm
& 7.30–11pm. Standard mid-
priced Portuguese grills served
in a characterful restaurant that
largely consists of a covered
patio. Live folk music on
Fridays.

Taska

Rua do Alportel 38 ☎ 289 824 739.
Mon–Sat noon–3pm & 7–11pm.
Friendly place serving traditional, moderately priced
Algarve fare to a mostly Portuguese crowd. House specialities
include *gambas* (prawns) accom-

▲MARINA-SIDE CAFÉ

panied by an excellent range of Portuguese regional wines.

Bars and clubs

Columbus
Jardim Manuel Bivar, corner with Rua João Dias ☎289 813 051. Tues–Sun 9.30pm–2am. Jazzy local haunt with seats outside under the arcades opposite the harbourfront gardens. There's a dartboard inside too.

Conselheiro
Rua Conselheiro Bivar 72–78 ☎289 803 191. Daily 10pm–4am. Disco bar with a minimum consumption of €25 most nights; indoor tables, swirling lights and occasionally some good tunes, together with karaoke on Wednesdays.

Gothic
Rua da Madelena 38 ☎289 807 887. Mon–Sat 11pm–4am. Goths are alive and still looking unwell at this suitably darkened club with cheap beer and wicked shots.

Millenium III
Rua do Prior 21 ☎289 823 628. Thurs–Sun 11pm–5am. Large industrial club playing all the latest sounds, good DJs and performances by local bands. One of the better venues in town.

Taberna da Sé
Largo da Sé 26 ☎965 827 662. Mon–Sat 10am–midnight. Arty tavern in the old town with outdoor tables attracting a friendly, young crowd. A popular spot for spontaneous jamming sessions on a summer's evening.

Upa Upa
Rua Conselheiro Bivar 51 ☎289 807 832. Daily 9pm–4am. Laid-back and relatively early-opening music bar with a mixed clientele; tables outside on the pedestrianized street.

West of Faro

Beyond Faro's international airport, Quinta do Lago and Vale do Lobo are relatively small resorts representing one of the most exclusive corners of the country. Studded with top golf courses and luxurious accommodation, this is where the likes of Michael Owen and Madonna choose to holiday amongst neatly tended semi-tropical gardens. Discrete, low-density villa complexes are served by a plethora of sports facilities and restaurants, though in an area where flash cars are the norm, there's little in the way of public transport. Indeed, the road to the area is a barely marked side-road from Almancil, whose church of São Laurenço has one of the most beautiful interiors in the country. Public transport improves around Vilamoura, a futuristic purpose-built resort, fronted by a superb beach that stretches west to the former fishing village of Olhas d'Água. Quarteira is the only town on this stretch that is unashamedly downmarket, with a fine beach and bustling market.

Almancil and the Igreja de São Laurenço

Regular buses from Faro throughout the day. Although Almancil itself is an undistinguished town, at its eastern edge is a hidden gem, the church of São Laurenço (☎289 395 451; Mon 2.30–6pm, Tues–Sat 10am–1pm & 2.30–6pm; €1.50). Built in the eighteenth century, the church survived the earthquake of 1755 and retains its superb, fully tiled interior depicting the life of São Laurenço (St Lawrence), in particular, panels

▼IGREJA DE SÃO LAURENÇO, ALMANCIL

▲DETAIL, IGREJA DE SÃO LAURENÇO

of his martyrdom showing his death in graphic detail. They were painted in 1730 by Policarpo de Oliveira Bernardes, considered one of the country's best artists.

Quinta do Lago

One to two daily buses from Loulé and Almancil. Fronted by a great beach and set amongst rolling grassland, waterways and pine forest, Quinta do Lago is Portugal's most upmarket purpose built resort. A sprawling, luxury holiday village linked by miles of roads and roundabouts, it boasts top-class golf courses (see p.191), a watersports complex, riding centre and opulent hotels. The main

car park is at the end of Avenida André Jorge, the main drag, from where a long wooden bridge crosses the Ria Formosa and dunes to the splendid sandspit beach, a huge swathe that is a continuation of Praia de Faro (see p.55). The area around the wooden bridge gets packed in high season, but just walk for ten minutes or so in either direction and you can find plenty of empty sand.

The sandspit also protects the eastern extremity of the Parque Natural da Ria Formosa, an important wetland area for birds and wildlife. Two well-used nature trails are signed from next to the bridge. The longer and marginally more appealing one, the São Laurenço *trilho*, heads southeast for an easy-to-follow 3.3km return walk past bird hides to a Roman pillar. The shorter 2.3km return walk, the Quinta do Lago *trilho*, heads northwest to a small lake where flamingos sometimes feed. The freshwater lagoon at Ludo just to the east is one of the few places in Portugal where you can see the purple galinule, one of the country's rarest species of bird.

▲BRIDGE TO THE BEACH, QUINTA DO LAGO

As you enter Quinta do Lago – at Roundabout 2 – there's a property sales office-cum-information centre (☎289 351 900, ⊛www.quintadolago.com; Mon–Fri 9.30am–1pm & 2.30–6pm), which can give out maps of the area.

Vale de Lobo

Served by two daily buses from Almancil. Vale de Lobo means "Valley of the Wolves", but there is little wildlife left here. The resort is similar to Quinta do Lago, with serious-money hotels and low-density upmarket villas. There is a 24-hour reception as you enter the complex (☎289 353 000, ⊛www.valedolobo.com), which can help with booking villas. Vale do Lobo is something of a prototype village which recently won a Green Globe award, a tourist industry prize for environmental awareness. The beach, Praia de Vale do Lobo, is a magnificent stretch of safe, soft sands with plenty of beach paraphernalia (sun loungers, umbrellas etc) for hire. First-rate sports facilities include nearby golf courses (see p.191) and the **Vale de Lobo Tennis Academy** (☎289 396 991), the most famous in the country, run by ex-Portuguese pro Pedro Frazão.

Quarteira

Quarteira has a very different feel to the deluxe resorts either side of it. It was one of the first former fishing villages to be developed in the Algarve, and remains high-rise and downmarket. Stick to the palm-lined seafront promenade and the attractive stretch of beach – Praia de Quarteira – and it's a pleasant enough destination, although a little way inland you're surrounded by rows of tower blocks. The town remains Portuguese in character, and there's a good weekly market each Wednesday just back from the tourist office – a section east of the bus station sells clothes, flowers and crafts. At other times, the town's main attraction is the bustling fish and vegetable **markets** (Mon–Sat 8am–3pm, Sun vegetable market only 8am–2pm) by the working

Visiting Quarteira

The bus terminus (☎289 389 143) is a couple of blocks back from the beach, on Avenida Dr. Sá Carneiro, with the turismo on Praça do Mar by the beach (May–Sept Mon & Fri–Sun 10am–1.30pm & 2.30–7pm, Tues–Thurs 9.30am–7pm; Oct–May same hours until 6pm; ☎289 389 209).

EATING & DRINKING		ACCOMMODATION	
Beira Mar	2	Dom José	C
O Jacinto	1	Miramar	B
Rosa Branca	3	Romeu	A

0	500 m

fishing harbour to the west end of town.

From May to September you can tour Quarteira on a **toy train** that trundles along the seafront and round

▼THE PROMENADE, QUARTEIRA

the town every hour or so (daily 10.15am–1pm & 3pm–midnight; €2).

Around Quarteira

Around 5km inland from Quarteira, on the crossroads between the EN125 and the road to Loulé at Quatro Estradas, the **Aqua Parque** water park (☎289 399 396; May–Sept daily 10am–6pm; €15) makes a fun excursion especially for those with kids, with various water chutes and slides. Nearby, **Vila Sol Morgadinhos** at Alto do Semino (see p.191) is one of the Algarve's less formal golf clubs, nicely situated amongst palm trees.

Vilamoura

Regular buses from Faro, Quarteira and Albufeira drop you next to the casino one block from the Praia da Marina, where there's plenty of car parking space. A short walk up the beach from Quarteira and based around Europe's largest marina stands Vilamoura, a modern and constantly expanding resort, with a bewildering

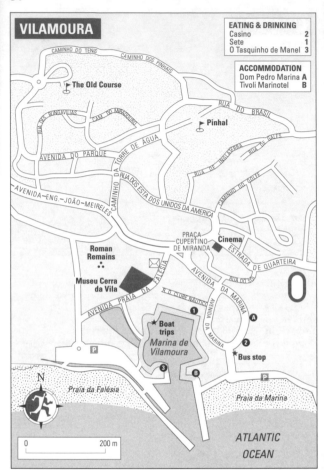

VILAMOURA

EATING & DRINKING
Casino 2
Sete 1
O Tasquinho de Manel 3

ACCOMMODATION
Dom Pedro Marina A
Tivoli Marinotel B

The Old Course

Pinhal

Roman Remains

Museu Cerra da Vila

Cinema

Boat trips

Marina de Vilamoura

Bus stop

Praia da Falésia

Praia da Marina

ATLANTIC OCEAN

0   200 m

network of almost 200km of roads. The resort was created in the 1970s as an upmarket extension of Quarteira, with around one hundred restaurants and shops and a few appealing trails over its red-sand cliffs for walking and cycling. Beyond the marina, the development radiates outwards with a series of low-density hotels and over a thousand villas set in sub-tropical grounds amongst top-notch golf courses.

Bristling with high-tech power boats and sleek yachts, the marina is the focus of the resort, surrounded by international cafés, bars and restaurants. At the northwest end, various stalls offer **boat trips** which range from dolphin-watching excursions to fishing trips and parascending; prices start from around €15 for a two-hour trip to €50 for a full-day excursion. The boat trips are a great way to see the cliffs, coves and

▲PRAIA DA FALÉSIA

beaches of the surrounding coastline.

East of the marina, the stunning Praia da Marina has two miles of soft, Blue Flag sands, though the crowds can get overwhelming in high season.

Vilamoura may be futuristic, but it was also an ancient settlement. The **Museu Cerra da Vila** (☎289 312 153; daily: May–Sept 10am–1pm & 3–8pm; Oct–April 9.30am–12.30pm & 2–6pm; €2) is an important archaeological site displaying the vestiges of a late Roman, Visigothic and Moorish colony. You can make out the foundations of a Roman mansion, baths and a fish-salting tank, together with well-preserved Roman mosaics. There's also a small exhibition hall on the site giving information about the history of the site.

Praia da Falésia

Praia da Falésia, a handsome stretch of sands backed by ochre-red sandstone cliffs (*falésias*) that give the beach its name, begins just west of Vilamoura marina. Getting there involves a short walk via a wooden footbridge over an inlet, so it's correspondingly less busy than the other beach on this stretch. Much of the dunes and cliffs here are part of the Parque Ambiental de Vilamoura, which has protected the beachside from the fairly uncontrolled development just back from the cliffs which stretches virtually all the way to Albufeira.

One of the nicest of the region's trails begins at the edge of Vilamoura's beach carpark, climbing the low, eroded cliffs, past spiky cactus plants, before rejoining the sands at the so-called Praia dos Tomates (Tomato Beach), where there is a seasonal café. Allow an hour for the full circuit.

Olhos de Água and Santa Eulalia

Served by regular bus from Albufeira. Olhos de Água, which translates as "eyes of the water", gets its name from the freshwater springs that bubble up under the sands. Its beach is broad, clean and alluring, though the once tiny fishing village is now all but engulfed by villas and restaurants tumbling down the steep slope to the coast.

At low tide you can walk the 2.5km from Olhos de Água along the beach to Praia da

▲ VILAMOURA MARINA

Oura, just 2km from Albufeira (see p.107). En route you pass Santa Eulalia, another fine beach dominated by a brand new spa complex.

Accommodation

Hotel Dom José

Avda Infance de Sagres, Quarteira ☎289 302 750, ⊛www.domjose-hotels.com. A high-rise three-star hotel right on the seafront, fairly characterless but very popular with package companies. The rooms are decently sized with satellite TV and a/c, and there's an in-house pool, bar and restaurant. Sea-view rooms cost €10 extra. €90.

Dom Pedro Marina

Avda Tivoli, Vilamoura ☎289 381 100, ⊛www.dompedro.com. This triangular-shaped pink block offers four-star facilities including a pool and restaurant. The best rooms have sea-facing terraces, the less expensive ones overlook a car park. €190.

Le Meridien Dona Filipa

Vale do Lobo ☎289 357 200, ⊛www .lemeridien-donafilipa.com. Five-star hotel near the beach in luxuriant landscaped grounds, which boast their own tennis courts. There are also restaurants, a children's club and special family activities in summer. €297.

Pensão Miramar

Rua Gonçalo Velho 8, Quarteira ☎289 315 225, ⊕289 314 671. Just off the seafront, this is much the best budget choice in town. The rooms are plain but spotless with private bathrooms and TVs. Some have sea views, others face a charming internal terrace. There's also a great communal roof terrace, and the price includes breakfast. €65.

Hotel Quinta do Lago

Quinta do Lago ☎289 350 350, ⊛www.quintadolagohotel.com. One of the country's top hotels and popular with celebrities who appreciate the privacy offered by its sprawling wooded grounds. Along with luxurious rooms, there are restaurants, bars, an indoor and outdoor pool, spa and sports facilities and discounts at the local golf courses. There are also eighteen family rooms. €485.

Pensão Romeu

Rua Gonçalo Velho 38, Quarteira ☏289 314 114. Up the road from the *Miramar* and almost identical in terms of its rooms and layout, though it lacks the sea views. Price incluces breakfast. €60.

Sheraton Pine Cliffs Algarve

Pinhal da Falésia ☏289 500 100, ⊛www.pinecliffs.com. Set in a wooded complex of villas and sports facilities just back from the cliffs between Vilamoura and Olhos de Água – with its own lift down to the beach – this is one of the classiest and priciest hotels in the Algarve. Rooms are huge and the best have balconies facing the sea. There are three pools (one indoors), a gym, tennis courts and discounts for the neighbouring golf course, plus disabled access. The grounds include the Porto Pirata, a self-contained children's village where parents can leave their kids in safe hands. €565.

Tivoli Marinotel

Vilamoura marina ☏289 303 303, ⊛www.tivolihotels.com. This concrete and glass high rise dominating the south side of the marina has nearly four hundred rooms, most with superb views over the neighbouring beach or marina, and facilities include indoor and outdoor pools, shops and restaurants. €326.

Campsite

Parque do Campiso

Quarteira ☏289 302 821, ☏289 302 822; booking for bungalows ☏218 117 070. A well-equipped campsite 1km east of town on the road to Almancil; any bus to or from Faro stops right outside. They also rent out rickety-looking two-tiered wooden bungalows

with their own bathrooms and kitchenettes sleeping two or four people from €66.

Cafés

Beira Mar

Avda Infante de Sagres 61, Quarteira. Mon–Sat 8am–midnight. This bustling *pastelaria* facing the beach makes a superb stop for breakfast or tea, its counter stuffed with sumptuous cakes and pastries.

Restaurants

O Jacinto

Avda Sá Carneiro, Quarteira ☏289 301 887. Tues–Thurs 10.30am–7pm, Fri 10.30am–6pm. Despite its relatively humble appearance, this is one of the best restaurants in the Algarve. Superbly cooked fish and seafood specialities include Quarteira prawns (around €70 a kilo). Reservations necessary.

La Cigale

Olhos de Água ☏289 501 637. Daily 10.30am–midnight. Highly rated seafood restaurant with an outdoor terrace facing the beach. The fish and seafood are expensive but not outrageously so, and few customers leave disappointed.

Rosa Branca

Marginal, Quarteira ☏289 314 430. Daily 10am–midnight. The best-positioned of a cluster of café-restaurants at the market end of the beach, with decently priced fish and grilled meats served on outdoor tables facing the sands.

O Tasquinho de Manel

Escola de Vela, Vilamoura. Tues–Sun noon–3pm & 7–11pm. On the way to Praia de Falésia, this simple

PLACES West of Faro

place lacks the pretensions of the marina-side restaurants. Just pick from the moderately priced fish in the counter and enjoy the view from the outdoor tables facing the marina.

Bars and clubs

Casino
Vilamoura ☎289 302 999. Daily 4pm–3am. Just south of the marina, Vilamoura's casino hosts a fairly tacky disco (June–Sept nightly; Oct–May Thurs–Sun 11pm–6am) and lays on regular cabaret-style dance shows and exhibitions.

Kadoc
Estrada de Vilamoura. June–Sept daily 11.30pm–6am; Oct–May Fri and Sat only. Entry from €10, depending on the night. Opposite the Mobil garage on the Vilamoura–Albufeira road, *Kadoc* is the Algarve's biggest club, pulling in up to eight thousand revellers a night, often with international guest DJs.

Sete
Bloco 7, Vilamoura marina ☎289 313 943. Daily 9am–3am. Fashionable chrome-and-steel café-bar part-owned by Portuguese soccer star Luís Figo and named after his shirt number (seven). By day it's a tranquil spot for a coffee or juice, but after dark the sound system cranks up. If you're lucky, one of Figo's mates may pop in – pictures on the wall show previous famous guests.

North of Faro

Though most people visit the Algarve for its beaches, it's well worth venturing inland to see some of the variety the region has to offer. Loulé is famed for its atmospheric Saturday market, while to the north stretches some of the Algarve's least spoilt countryside. Here, the Serra do Caldeirão, dotted with olive and citrus groves, separates the Algarve from the neighbouring region of the Alentejo. Many of its rolling hills are given over to subsistence farming, with the fields and orchards worked as they have been for centuries. This countryside is beautiful terrain for a walk or picnic, especially around the tiny villages of Benafim, Penina and Salir, the latter with the remains of a Moorish castle. Ringed by cork woods, São Bras de Alportel is a sleepy market town with an attractive *pousada* and a quirky museum, while Estói boasts the beautiful gardens of the Palácio de Estói and the fascinating Roman site of Milreu.

Loulé centre

Loulé has always been an important market town, and though its modern suburbs sprawl over the surrounding hills, its compact centre doesn't take long to look around. Its most interesting streets, a grid of whitewashed cobbled lanes, lie between the remains of its Moorish castle (now a museum) and the thirteenth-century Gothic Igreja Matriz church, with its tall belltower and palm-lined gardens in front. Here you'll see workshops of traditional craftsmen producing leatherwork and copper *cataplanas* (cooking vessels).

Loulé market

Loulé's most atmospheric sight is the wonderful covered fruit and vegetable *mercado* (market) (Mon–Sat 8am–3pm), set in a red onion-domed building with Moorish keyhole-style windows. Try and visit on a Saturday morning, when the market spreads into the surrounding streets – a medley of stalls selling everything from pungent cheeses to cages of live chickens and rabbits. Close by, on Avenida Marçal Pacheco, one block beyond the market, check out the Manueline carvings of coiled ropes on the facade of the Misericordia church.

▲FRUIT AND VEGETABLE MARKET, LOULÉ

Loulé: Museu Arqueológico and the castle

Rua D.Paio Peres Correia 17 ☎289 400 642. Mon–Thurs 9am–5.30pm, Sat 10am–2pm. €1.10. The remains of Loulé's castle enclose a small but interesting Museu Arqueológico, housing a range of Roman, Moorish and early Portuguese finds from Loulé and the surrounding area. There are second-century amphora, ninth-century pots from Salir castle (see p.72) and the foundations of a twelfth-century Moorish house, in situ under a glass floor. The largest exhibit is a giant sixteenth-century stone urn, retrieved from the castle itself.

The entry price to the museum allows access to the castle walls, from where you can gaze down over the old town and, on a clear day, right down to the coast. The entrance is up the steps to the side of the museum, via a kitchen set out in traditional Algarvian style, complete with pots, pans and straw dummies in traditional dress.

Loulé: Saturday market and Nossa Senhora da Piedade

Loulé's Saturday morning (from 9.30am) gypsy market is one of the most colourful in the Algarve. It takes place around fifteen minutes' walk northwest of the centre – follow the signs to IP1/Boliquieme – on a patch of ground beautifully framed by a pair of dazzling white

Visiting Loulé

The bus terminal (☎289 416 655/6) is on Rua Nossa Senhora de Fátima, a couple of minutes' walk north from the old town; there are daily services from Quarteira, Albufeira and Faro. The turismo (May–Sept Mon–Fri 9.30am–7pm, Sat 10am–6pm; Oct–April Mon–Fri 9.30am–5.30pm, Sat 10am–2pm; ☎289 463 900) is due to move from its position inside the castle walls to an office on Avenida 25 de Abril, close to the park, by 2005. A good time to visit Loulé is in July, when it hosts an annual Jazz Festival featuring top international musicians at weekends.

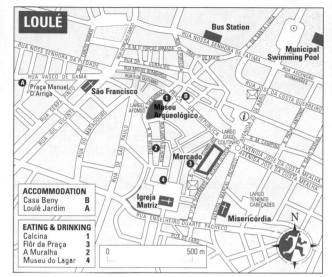

churches. Stalls sell a motley collection of clothes, ceramics, agricultural produce and general goods, with a separate section selling plants and flowers over the road – though much of the colour comes from the market traders themselves.

The market is peered over by the beehive-shaped Nossa Senhora da Piedade – steps wind up to its hilltop position from the far side of the market. At Easter, the church is the starting point of a procession into town for **Mãe Soberana**, one of the Algarve's most important religious festivals (see p.189).

Querença and Salir

Ten kilometres northeast of Loulé, Querença is an unexceptional village that comes alive in January for a Smoked

▼VIEW FROM CASTLE WALLS, LOULÉ

▲ERMIDA DE PÉ DA CRUZ, SALIR

Sausage Fair (see p.190). Of more interest at other times is the attractive agricultural village of Salir. Set on a hilltop facing rolling countryside, Salir retains the vestiges of a Moorish castle. To visit, park by the diminutive Ermida de Pé da Cruz church; from here it's a short stroll along a cobbled track to what's left of the castle – a few low walls and the remains of turrets. Though the ruins are no great shakes, they're in a gorgeous position, the path passing white flower-decked houses with great views over Salir and the valley beyond.

Benafim and Penina

One daily return bus from Loulé, continuing to Alte (see p.113). The pretty village of Benafim is a maze of whitewashed houses and narrow streets sitting in the heart of some of the least spoilt parts of the region. For a real taste of rural Algarve, take the signed back road from Benafim, which leads to Penina before rejoining the main road at the village of Pena – a short drive or a superb eight-kilo-metre-round walk, returning to Benafim along the main EN124. En route you'll pass through cork and olive groves dotted with traditional wells.

Penina itself is a simple agricultural village where some of the elderly inhabitants still wear traditional dress, with one drink spot, the *Café Cacadores* (open daily), close to the main shop.

Rocha da Pena

Beyond Penina, the road contin-ues alongside the foot of Rocha da Pena, a craggy limestone hill protecting rare flora and fauna, including mongoose, eagle owls, buzzards and Bonelli eagles. You'll need to walk to the hill itself for a likely chance to see any of these – there's a way-marked trail across it from near Pena, another totally unspoilt, tiny, agricultural village.

São Brás de Alportel

Though hardly the region's most attractive town, São Bras de Alportel makes a good stop to stretch your legs. Just east of the main square, on Rua Dr. José Dias Sancho 61, the **Museu Etnográfico do Trajo Algarvio** (℗289 840 100, ⓦwww.museu-trajo-algarve. web.pt; Mon–Fri 10am–1pm & 2–5pm, Sat 2–5pm; €1), housed in an old mansion, is the best reason to come to São Brás, its alcoves and corridors full of tra-ditional costumes. At the back, a series of buildings round a courtyard contain cork-cutting equipment, ancient donkey car-riages, saddles, bull carts and an

Visiting São Bras de Alportel

Regular buses from Faro pull into the main square, Largo São Sebastião, a fairly dull space with a couple of banks. There's a small tourist office at no. 23 (☏289 843 165, ✉turismo.saobras@rtalgarve.pt; Mon–Fri 10am–1.30pm & 2.30–6pm), which can give out maps of the town.

old loom. Occasional demonstrations of the machinery take place and, outside in the courtyard, you can walk down steps to the bottom of a traditional well which has been partly excavated.

From the museum, cut down Rua Nova de Fonte and you'll reach the **Jardim da Verbena** (May–Sept 8am–8pm; Oct–April 8am–5pm; free), a wonderful little garden with an open-air swimming pool (hours as park; free). Just west of here lie the narrow streets of the oldest part of town, clustered round the church of Senhor dos Passos (signposted Igreja Matriz), from where there are lovely views of the surrounding valleys.

Palácio do Visconde de Estói

Regular buses from Faro. While Estói itself is a typical nondescript inland village, it's famous for the delightful peach-coloured Palácio do Visconde de Estói, now a *pousada* (hotel). This is a diminutive version of the Rococo palace of Queluz near Lisbon, built by the Visconde de Carvalha at the end of the eighteenth century. Its attractive *jardim* (garden), reached down a palm-lined avenue near the attractive Igreja Matriz church, is open to the public (Mon–Sat 9am–12.30pm & 2–5.30pm; free). The grounds spread down below a terrace dotted with statues of Portuguese literary figures – Camões, Herculano and Garrett – along with the Marquês de Pombal,

who helped rebuild much of the country after the Great Earthquake of 1755. Look out, too, for some beautiful eighteenth-century *azulejos* of plants and tropical birds.

Milreu

Rua de Faro ☏289 997 823, ⊛www .ippar.pt. Tues–Sun: April–Sept 9.30am–12.30pm & 2–6pm; Oct–March 9.30am–12.30pm & 2–5pm. €2. The Roman site at Milreu, a ten-minute walk downhill from Estói's main square, is one of the most important Roman sites in

▼THE GATE TO PALÁCIO DO VISCONDE DE ESTÓI

Portugal. It predated Faro and was inhabited from the second to the sixth century AD. The site is relatively small and it's easy to find your way around. Archaeological excavations are ongoing, but you can clearly make out the remains of a peristyle villa to the north of the site, dominated by the apse of a temple a little to the south, which was converted into a Christian basilica in the third century AD, making it one of the earliest known Christian churches in the world. The other recognizable remains are of a bathing complex southwest of the villa, which had underfloor heating, with fragments of fish mosaics; and the apodyterium, or changing room, with its stone benches and arched niches below for clothes. Many of the busts from the site – including those of Hadrian and Empress Agrippina Minor – are on display in Faro's archaeological museum (see p.53).

Accommodation

Casa Beny

Rua de São Domingos 13, Loulé ☎289 417 702. A tastefully renovated town house offering plush rooms, with their own cable TV and bathroom. The roof terrace has great views over the main street – which can be noisy. €50.

Loulé Jardim Hotel

Praça Manuel de Arriaga 23, Loulé ☎289 413 094, ℱ289 463 177. Facing a quiet square, this friendly and attractive hotel has small but well-decorated en-suite rooms, each with cable TV. There's also a bar and a small rooftop pool, while breakfast is a fine buffet spread of fruit, breads and preserves. €70.

Pousada de São Brás

São Bras de Alportel ☎289 845 171, ✉enatur@mail.telepac.pt. Terracotta-tiled 1940s building set on a hillside 2km north of São Bras de Alportel. The views from the comfortable rooms' balconies are splendid, and there's a pool, tennis courts, games room and expensive restaurant (see opposite). Advance booking essential in summer; rates tumble in winter. €134.

Residencial São Brás

Rua Luís Bivar 27, São Bras de Alportel ☎ & ℱ289 842 213. An attractive town house with an ornate stairway a couple of minutes' walk west of the main square, swathed in *azulejos*. Sadly, the large, musty rooms don't live up to the communal areas, and bathrooms are shared. €60.

▼THE ROMAN SITE OF MILREU

Cafés

Café Calcina
Praça da República, Loulé, Mon–Sat 8am–11.30pm. A highly atmospheric little café with marble tabletops and black-and-white photos of old Loulé on the walls. The perfect spot for *pastéis de nata* (custard cream tarts), *rissóis de bacalhau* (dried cod rissoles) or a beer with *tremoços* (pickled lupin seeds).

Mouro Bar Castelo
Rua dos Muros do Castelo 1, Salir. Tues–Sun noon–10pm. This simple café-bar near Salir castle serves drinks and Portuguese nosh at decent prices; the dining room commands superb views over the valley.

Restaurants

Casa do Pasto Victor's
Rua Vasco da Gama 41, Estói. Mon–Sat noon–3pm & 7–10pm. Just off the square on the Olhão road, this is a cheap and cheerful grill house where you'd be hard pushed to spend more than €8 a head.

Flôr da Praça
Rua José Fernandes Guerreiro 44, Loulé ☎289 462 435. Mon–Sat 12.30–2.30pm & 7.30–11.30pm. Bargain fish and grills are served in this large, characterful restaurant opposite the market, its walls decorated with old photos, seashells and soccer memorabilia. Full meals around €10.

A Muralha
Rua Martim Moniz 39, Loulé ☎289 412 629. Mon–Fri 7–11pm, Sat noon–3pm & 7–11pm. With a flower-filled patio and *azulejo* panels of old Loulé decorating the interior, this is one of the most popular tourist spots in town. Grills are moderately priced but unexceptional, while the pricier, more elaborate meat and seafood dishes such as *arroz de marisco* and meat fondues are good bets. There's also a children's menu, and live music on Saturday evenings.

Museu do Lagar
Largo da Matriz 7, Loulé ☎289 416 307. Tues–Sun noon–4pm & 7–11pm. Opposite the Igreja Matriz, this cavernous and very expensive *marisqueria* has its own fountain and bubbling fish tanks. A good range of well-prepared dishes include mixed meat kebabs and seafood *cataplana*.

Pousada de São Brás
São Bras de Alportel ☎289 845 1712. Daily noon–2.30pm & 7.30–9pm. This *pousada* restaurant commands superb views over the surrounding valleys. International and Portuguese cuisine is well prepared and not too outrageously priced (unlike the wine list), though some may find the service overly formal. Book ahead in summer.

Savoy
Rua Luís Bivar 40, São Bras de Alportel Mon, Tues and Thurs–Sun 6–11pm. Past the *Residencial São Brás*, this good-value option serves old-fashioned international cuisine such as prawn cocktail, spaghetti bolognese and pork with apple sauce. There's also a kids' menu.

Olhão and around

Olhão is an unspoilt and characterful town with attractive riverside gardens, a kernel of Moorish-style houses and a great market. Olhão's harbour is protected by two sandspit islands, Ilha da Culatra and Ilha da Armona, with superb Atlantic-facing beaches. The latter can also be reached from Fuzeta, a delightful fishing village with its own river beach. The *ilhas* protect a marshy lagoon, part of the Reserva Natural da Ria Formosa, which can be visited from Quinta da Marim, an environmental centre that's home to bizarre aquatic poodles.

Olhão

Once through the built-up outskirts, Olhão is an attractive town. While there are no

▼FISHERMAN, OLHÃO

sights as such, the warren of narrow streets and flat roofs of the old town give a striking North African feel to the place. Indeed, Olhão has centuries-old trading links with Morocco. The town's most prominent building is the unspectacular seventeenth-century parish church of **Nossa Senhora do Rosário** (daily 9am–noon & 3–6pm). Outside, at the back of the church, an iron grille protects the chapel of Nossa Senhora dos Aflitos, where townswomen traditionally gathered to pray for their menfolk when there was a storm out at sea. Nowadays curious wax models of children and limbs sit amid candles as ex voto offerings for fertility and to cure ailments.

The other obvious focus of the town is the **market** (Mon–Fri 7am–2pm, Sat 6.30am–3pm), held in the two modern red-brick turreted buildings on the harbour at the

Visiting Olhão

The train station lies at the northeastern edge of town, off Avenida dos Combatentes da Grande Guerra, some ten to fifteen minutes' walk from the waterfront. The bus terminal (☏289 702 157) is a few minutes away on Rua General Humberto Delgado. The turismo, on Largo Sebastião Martins Mestre (☏289 713 936; June to mid-Sept daily 9.30am–7pm; mid-Sept to May Mon–Fri 10am–1.30pm & 2.30–6pm), can advise on accommodation and give boat times to the *ilhas*. There's also a timetable for ferry services to both islands posted at the ticket kiosk by the quayside; if it's closed you can buy tickets on the ferries.

PLACES Olhão and around

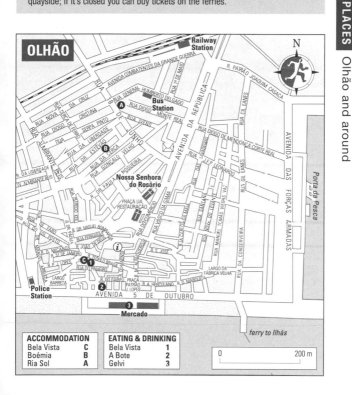

OLHÃO

ACCOMMODATION		EATING & DRINKING	
Bela Vista	C	Bela Vista	1
Boémia	B	A Bote	2
Ria Sol	A	Gelvi	3

bottom of town. There's meat, fruit and vegetables and cheeses on one side, fish on the other. The fish hall is full of such delights as octopus, scabbard fish and the ubiquitous sardine.

Either side of the market lie shady riverside gardens, complete with kids' play areas and a miniature aviary.

Ilha da Culatra

Ferries from Olhão depart to the Ilha da Culatra throughout the year (June & Sept 6 daily; July & Aug 7 daily; rest of year 4 daily; €2 to Culatra, €2.60 to Farol return), calling at Culatra (35min) and Farol (45min). In summer, an additional service runs between Farol and Faro (see p.55). The Ilha da Culatra is the most populated of the sandspits, its northern, land-

▲THE LIGHTHOUSE AT FAROL

facing shore dotted with a series of fishermen's huts between the two main centres at either end of the island, Culatra and Farol. In summer the island's population swells to around three thousand, well supported by a mini market, medical centre and a cluster of seasonal cafés. The easternmost of the settlements is the ferry's first port of call, **Culatra**, the larger of the two, a fairly untidy collection of huts and holiday homes. Ten minutes west by boat, **Farol**, the second stop, is far more agreeable. A network of narrow paths links low-rise holiday homes and fishermen's huts clustered round a tall *farol* (lighthouse). Like Culatra, Farol is edged by beautiful tracts of beach on the ocean side, though the mainland-facing beach is grubby. In winter the villages are almost deserted.

If you want to stay on Culatra, ask around at the cafés for private rooms; camping on the island is not encouraged.

Ilha da Armona

Boats run from Olhão all year round (June & early Sept 9 departures daily; July & Aug first departure 7.30am, then hourly 9am–8pm; late Sept–May 4 daily). 15min; €2 return. Faced by miles of attractive, dune-backed sands, Armona is a very popular summer destination, though it doesn't take much of a walk up the sands to get away from the crowds. Ferries drop their passengers at the northern end of the single settlement on Ilha da Armona – a long strip of holiday chalets and huts that stretches right across the island on either side of the main path. Follow the path and it's a fifteen-minute walk to the ocean-facing beach. You can walk along the usually deserted sands from the Olhão end of Armona to the eastern end opposite Fuzeta in about two hours. For details of Praia da Fuzeta, see p.80.

There are a few bar-restaurants by the jetty, though most close out of season, when it is best to stock up on supplies from Olhão's market.

Quinta da Marim

Daily: visitor centre 9.30am–12.30pm & 2.30–5.30pm; park: June–Sept 8am–8pm; Oct–May 8am– 6pm. €1.50. Served by regular bus from Olhão and Fuzeta, Quinta da Marim is an environmental educational centre within the **Parque Natural da Ria Formosa** in an atmospheric area of scrubby dunes and mud flats dotted with pines and gorse. The reserve is best known for being the refuge for bizarre aquatic poodles, dogs that were bred to dive into the water to help chase fish into the fishermen's nets. Unfortunately, the aquatic poodles were abandoned for more modern methods in the 1950s, though these shaggy dogs still thrive here in their purebred form. The poodles can be seen as part of a three-kilometre-long nature trail that leads from the car park past various signed highlights: a salt marsh, a freshwater pond where you sometimes can spot rare birds – including, if you're lucky, the rare purple galinule – a bird hospital and the remains of Roman salting tanks, used for preserving fish. The highlight, at the waterfront, is one of Portugal's last working *moinhos de maré* (tidal mills), a lovely whitewashed building with a fine organic café and handicrafts shop on its flat roof (daily 10am–5pm).

In the middle of the park, a visitor centre has models of traditional fishing boats, fossils, a small aquarium of native fish

and a decent café, as well as a roof terrace from where you can admire storks nests in early summer.

Fuzeta

Fuzeta (or Fuseta) is one of the Algarve's least "discovered" resorts, probably because of its shortage of accommodation. It is not the region's most beautiful town, but it does retain its character as a working fishing village. Indeed, its daily routine revolves round the fishermen – whose colourful boats line the river alongside town – and, in summer, the central campsite and its lively community of backpackers. The two communities usually mingle at a line of lively café-bars in kiosks spreading down from the ferry stop towards the river beach.

The town's straggle of back-streets sit on a low hill facing the lagoon, sheltered by the eastern extremity of Ilha da Armona. Its waterfront of modern shops and apartments faces broad gardens largely taken over by the campsite. Beyond this lies a river beach, a fine bendy stretch of white sands weaving up to a wooden lifeboat house. In summer many people splash about in the calm waters of the river, though more exhilarating and cleaner waters can be had over the river at Praia da Fuzeta on the Ilha da Armona (see p.80).

Many of the local fish find their way to the small covered market on Largo 1° de Maio, the road running parallel to the river; the quayside behind the building is often lined with drying octopus. On Saturdays the

▼QUINTA DA MARIM

▲FUZETA WATERFRONT

market expands into a weekly flea market that lines the adjacent pedestrianized Rua Tenente Barrosa. At other times, everyday goods can be bought from shops around the town's pretty little palm tree-lined central square and Rua da Liberdade, the main shopping Street.

Praia da Fuzeta

Regular ferries (April–Oct roughly every fifteen minutes from 9am to 7pm and often later at busy times; Nov–March four daily; check with the ferryman what time the last return leaves; €1.10 return) shuttle from the fishing quay at the back of Fuzeta's campsite to the beach across the lagoon. The narrow Praia da Fuzeta on the eastern end of the Ilha da Armona (see p.78) is one of the nicest of the Algarve's sandspit beaches. The beach immediately opposite the ferry stop gets fairly crowded in high summer, but you only have to

walk ten minutes or so either way from the holiday beach huts and seasonal drinks kiosks to have beautiful, low dune-backed sands all to yourself.

Accommodation

Pensão Bela Vista

Rua Teófilo Braga 65–67, Olhão ☎ & ℱ289 702 538. The best budget option in town. The reception is spotless and the bright rooms, most en suite, are arranged around a tiled, flower-filled courtyard. Booking advisable. €40.

Pensão Boémia

Rua da Cerca 20, off Rua 18 de Junho, Olhão ☎ & ℱ289 714 513. This neat place offers appealing en-suite rooms with balconies. It's slightly out of the centre, near the post office, and handy for the bus station. €35.

Visiting Fuzeta

Fuzeta is on the main Faro–Vila Real train line; the station is ten minutes' walk from the waterfront, at the northern end of Rua da Liberdade. Regular buses from Olhão pull up at the waterfront opposite the campsite.

Monte Alegre

Apartadeo 64, Fuzeta ☏289 794
222, ✉monte.alegre@iol.pt. Set in
countryside with great coastal
views, around 2km north-
west of Fuzeta – signed Bias
Sul – *Monte Alegre* consists of
three well-equipped apartments sleeping up to five, and
a superb double room with its
own terrace. Run by a friendly
German family, there's an
outdoor swimming pool, stables
for horse rides and a pond full
of resident frogs; rooms all have
satellite TV and kitchenettes.
From €80.

Orbitur Armona

Ilha da Armona. April–Oct only ☏289
714 173. The only overnight
options on the island are the
simple holiday bungalows let
out by *Orbitur*, each with their
own bathrooms. Book ahead in
high season. €56.

Hotel Ria Sol

Rua General Humberto Delgado 37,
Olhão ☏289 705 267, ✆289 705 268.
Recently renovated, this standard two-star hotel is just up
from the bus station. All rooms
are clean, en suite and with TVs,
and there's a lively downstairs
bar. €70.

Campsites

Parque de Campismo da Fuzeta

Rua da Liberdade, Fuzeta ☏289 793
459, ✆289 794 034. Beautifully
positioned site under trees with
its own mini market, but it gets
pretty chock-a-block in high
summer.

Parque de Campismo de Olhão

Pinheiros de Marim ☏289 700 300,
✆www.sbsi.pt/camping. Served by

regular bus from Olhão, this
upmarket campsite opposite
Quinta da Marim is set in substantial grounds with its own
pool, kids' playground, tennis
courts, mini market, restaurant
and bars; there is even live music
some nights.

Cafés

Café Gelvi

Mercado, Avda 5 de Outubro, Olhão.
Tues–Sun 8am–midnight. Bustling
pastelaria, *geladaria* and *crois-
santeria* in the corner of the
fish market, with outdoor seats
facing the water.

Café das Taças

Rua da Liberdade 33, Fuzeta ☏289
793 038. Daily 8am–9pm. In a
great building with a Moorish
keyhole-shaped door and
window, this characterful
place serves superb coffee and
big fluffy croissants; there are
outdoor tables on the main
street.

Restaurants

Bela Vista

Rua Dr Teofilio Braga 59, Olhão ☏917
879 361. Mon–Sat 8am–11pm. Close
to the tourist office, this simple,
low-ceilinged café-restaurant
with blue *azulejos* is a cosy and
inexpensive place for generous
portions of grilled meats and
fish.

A Bote

Avda 5 de Outubro 122, Olhão ☏289
721 183. Mon–Sat 11am–4pm & 7pm–
midnight. A bustling restaurant,
close to the fish market, serving
mid-priced grilled fish and
meat, accompanied by mounds
of potatoes and salad.

O Caetano

Praia da Fuzeta, Ilha de Armona ☎919 962 048. Daily: May–Sept 9.30am–7pm; Oct–April 9.30am–5pm. Just by the ferry stop, this is Praia da Fuzeta's only restaurant, though it often runs out of food by 4pm; get there early for superb salads and well-priced fish and meat dishes. Also serves snacks and drinks on a small shady outdoor terrace.

Capri

Praça da República 4, Fuzeta ☎289 793 165. Mon, Tues & Thurs–Sun 10am–midnight. Lively bar-restaurant with tables on the main square. Simple, inexpensive dishes include hit-and-miss fish of the day and more reliable grills.

Bars

Bar Beira Mar 18

Fuzeta. Mon–Sat 7am–midnight. Opposite the ferry stop, this wooden shack with a few outdoor tables is where the fishermen enjoy their Super Bock beers from dawn onwards. Always lively and usually packed with locals, it also does simple meals.

Tavira and around

Despite its inland position, Tavira has become a bustling resort. Set on both sides of the gently flowing Rio Gilão, its highly picturesque old town is a graceful ensemble of church spires and eighteenth-century, crumbling white mansions with hipped terracotta roofs and wrought-iron balconies. There is the inevitable ring of new apartments radiating outwards, but the atmosphere is enhanced by a lively fishing trade along the riverfront. Most visitors are lured here by the spectacular local sandspit beach, the Ilha de Tavira – the fact that it can only be reached by ferry or by toy train adds to the fun. A more traditional village is nearby too, in the atmospheric fishing port of Santa Luzia, known as the capital of the octopus.

Igreja da Misericórdia

Of Tavira's 37 churches, the recently restored facade of the Igreja da Misericórdia, just up from the tourist office, is of most interest, a fine example of the Manueline style of architecture. Built between 1541 and 1551 by André Pilarte, the mason who worked on Belém's famous Jeronimos monastery in Lisbon, the church's carved stone doorway depicts a series of mermaids, angels and saints, including Peter and Paul, though the most visible carvings are a couple of lute-playing

Visiting Tavira

Tavira's bus terminal (☏ 281 322 546) is by the river, two minutes' walk to the main square, Praça da República, while the train station lies 1km south of the square. Up the steps just off Praça da República is the turismo, at Rua da Galeria 9 (☏ 281 322 511; daily: May–Oct 10am–1pm & 2–6pm; Nov–April 9.30am–1pm & 2–6pm). Arriving by car, there is a complicated one-way system in the central area; it is best to head for the free carpark under the flyover taking traffic east; follow signs to Quatro Águas (which is reached by heading under the flyover and following the river). A fun way to get your bearings of the town is by taking the toy train, which does a circuit daily every 45 minutes (10am–dusk; €2.50) out to the ferry jetty at Quatro Águas. Alternatively, Sport Nautica, Rua J. Pessoa 26 (☏ 281 324 943), offers bike hire from €5 a day.

figures in the doorframe. The striking *azulejo*-lined interior (open just before and after Mass) shows scenes from the life of Christ, below an impressive wooden vaulted ceiling.

The castle

The ruins of the Castelo (Mon–Fri 8am–5pm, Sat & Sun 9am–5.30pm; free) lie half hidden amid landscaped gardens. There has been a fort here since Phoenician times, though the current structure dates from the thirteenth century, and parts were rebuilt in the seventeenth century. From the walls there are great views over the distinctive curved terracotta rooftops and the town's many churches.

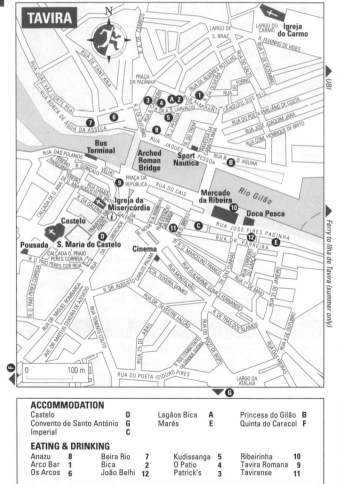

Santa Maria do Castelo

The impressively large and whitewashed church of Santa Maria do Castelo was built in the thirteenth century and restructured in the eighteenth century in Renaissance style. It contains the tomb of Dom Paio Peres Correia, who reconquered much of the Algarve from the Moors, including Tavira itself in 1242. Fittingly, the church stands on the site of the former mosque. Opposite, the former Convento da Nossa Senhora da Graça is due to open as a *pousada*.

The riverfront

With its tranquil vistas and palm-lined gardens, the riverfront is the best part of Tavira for a wander. Apart from the pedestrianized bridge – parts of which date back to Roman times – and the austere Carmelite church **Igreja do Carmo**, which holds a famous Christmas concert – there are no sights as such north of the river, though the old streets hide many of the town's best restaurants. South of the river, the former town market building, **Mercado da Riberia**, has become a "cultural centre" – actually a handful of small boutiques and appealing waterfront cafés. The old market walls are also used for temporary exhibitions, usually the works of local artists and photographers.

Past the fish market – for the trade only – fishing boats dock as far as the new flyover; appropriately, along this stretch of river lie various slightly pricey and touristy fish restaurants. Just before the flyover, **ferries** depart for the beach (see p.86). Head

▲ TAVIRA ROOFTOPS

under the bridge and you'll see the large new town **market** (Mon–Sat 8am–1.30pm) it's housed in a dull concrete box but has a wonderfully atmospheric and bustling interior, filled with a huge array of fruit and vegetables.

Ilha de Tavira

At some 14km in length and backed by nothing but tufted dunes, the beach at the **Ilha de Tavira** is one of the most spectacular in the entire Algarve.

In high summer, the nearest stretch of beach to the ferry terminal is packed with families and a largely Portuguese crowd, though you only have to walk fifteen minutes or so to be clear of the crowds, and out of season you'll probably have the place entirely to yourself.

To get to the beach, head down the path which runs from

▲ILHA DE TAVIRA

the jetty through a small chalet settlement, and you'll find beach umbrellas, pedaloes and half a dozen bar-restaurants.

Vila Galé Albacora and the tuna fishing museum

Museum: Daily 10am–6pm. Free.
East of the Rio Gilão opposite Quatro Águas, the plush *Vila Galé Albacora* hotel (see p.89). was built in the 1940s as a self-contained fishing village, where tuna fishermen spent the season with their families. The small but informative museum here shows how important tuna was to the area. Until the mid twentieth-century, fleets of forty or so boats set up in formation known as an *armação* designed to guide tuna into the centre of a system of nets. The best ever catch was in 1881, when 43,000 tuna were netted, but by the 1970s, the annual catch dwindled to just one tuna and the industry collapsed. Today, former houses have been turned into rooms, though the village's chapel is still used, and the former school is now a children's club. The route to the hotel passes a series of *salinas*, salt extraction plants which supply fifty percent of Portugal's salt using an evaporation system that has little changed since Roman times.

Santa Luzia

Santa Luzia is an earthy working fishing village with a number of seafood restaurants catering to day-trippers attracted by its palm-lined waterfront. The main catch here is octopus, and you'll see octopus traps lining the

Visiting Ilha de Tavira

Direct ferries (July–Sept: daily 8.30am–8pm, roughly hourly. €1.50 return) serve the island from Tavira's riverfront (see p.85). Alternatively, you can take a toy train (see p.87) or a bus (July to mid-Sept Mon–Fri roughly hourly) from the bus station in Tavira, for the ten-minute trip (or half-hour walk) to the jetty at Quatro Águas. From here, ferries (Easter–June 8am–8pm; July–Sept 8am–9pm; Oct–Easter 9am–dusk; €1 return) take just five minutes. The frequency of the service tends to depend on how busy things are: in high season they run every fifteen minutes or so, often until much later than 9pm; at other times they run roughly hourly; check with the ferryman what time the last boat returns. Alternatively, aquataxis (daily from 8am, ☎964 515 073) do the ride for €6 for up to six people.

small but lively fishing harbour. If you want to get out to the Ilha de Tavira from here (see p.85), Safari Boats (☎917 286 382) offer excursions, usually on Tuesdays and Thursdays.

Cascatas Moinhos da Rocha

Set in bucolic countryside 7km north of Tavira, the *cascatas* (waterfalls) of Moinhos da Rocha are a popular summer picnic spot for Portuguese families. A series of wooden decks and bridges skirt a leafy ravine sheltering the crystal-clear waters of a small stream. This culminates in a low but nevertheless impressive waterfall that empties into a little lake – it's used as a water source, so avoid swimming in it.

Pedras d'el Rei and Praia de Barril

Served by six buses daily from Tavira's bus station (Mon–Fri only). *Pedras d'El Rei* is a fairly upmarket holiday complex (see p.88) which offers access to another stretch of the Ilha da Tavira at Barril. From the bus stop and car park next to *Pedras d'El Rei*, cross the causeway to the termi-nal of a rather ancient-looking **miniature train** (daily, except in bad weather, 8am–dusk, roughly every 15–30min; €1 single, free to *Pedras d'El Rei* guests). This shuttles across the mud flats – past thousands of fiddler crabs – to the beach of **Barril** on the Ilha de Tavira. You can also walk alongside the tracks in ten to fifteen minutes. At the beach, attractive houses once belonging to fishermen have been turned into a cluster of slightly pricey café-restaurants; there's also a small shop, showers and toilets. A few minutes' walk right or left of the terminus – past lines of rusting anchors wedged into the dunes – and there are miles of beautiful, dune-fringed beach.

Accommodation

Pensão do Castelo

Rua da Liberdade 22, Tavira ☎281 320 790, ☎281 320 799. Rambling, very centrally located place, offering enormous clean rooms all with marble floors, TVs and bathrooms; the front rooms can be noisy. Disabled access. €60.

▼RELICS OF THE TUNA FISHING INDUSTRY, BARRIL

PLACES Tavira and around

▲THE ROMAN BRIDGE, TAVIRA

Convento de Santo António

Rua de Santo António, Tavira.
☎281 321 573, ℻281 325 632.
Closed Jan. With just seven
double rooms and a "superior"
chapel room, it is best to book
ahead (fax only) to bag a place
in this elegant sixteenth-century
convent with roof terrace.
There's also a swimming pool,
and breakfast is served in the
tranquil courtyard. Minimum
stay of four nights in summer;
two in winter. €150.

Residencial Imperial

Rua José Pires Padinha 24, Tavira ☎
& ℻281 322 234. Small *residencial*
with attached restaurant; the nicest rooms overlook the gardens
and river. All rooms have TV and
shower, though they're on the
small side. €55.

Residencial Lagâos Bica

Rua Almirante Cândido dos Reis 24,
Tavira ☎281 322 252. Characterful
place on the north side of the
river with small, simple en-suite
rooms clustered round a patio.
There's also a communal roof
terrace. Price does not include
breakfast. €40.

Residencial Marés

Rua José Pires Padinha
134–140, Tavira ☎281 325 815,
✉maresresidencial@mail.telepac
.pt. Twenty-four spotless rooms,
some on the small side but all
with a/c, TVs, *azulejos* and some
with balconies over the river or
old town. There's a great roof
terrace and a communal sauna
too. €80.

Pedras d'el Rei

☎281 380 600, ⊕www.pedrasdelrei
.com. Perfect for families, this
well-established holiday village
consists of a series of spacious
apartments and villas set in
beautifully landscaped grounds.
There's a central lawned area
focused on an outdoor pool and
overlooked by a café, bar and a
restaurant. Facilities include a
playground, children's club, and
well-stocked shop; there's also
an aviary, and residents have free
passes for the train to the beach.
Apartments from €96.

Residencial Princesa do Gilão

Rua Borda d'Àgua de Aguiar 10–12,
Tavira ☎ & ℻281 325 171. This
friendly *residencial* stands right on
the quayside, a modern, white
building with *azulejo*-decorated
interior. Rooms are tiny but have
their own shower rooms and
small balconies (those at the front
overlook the river). €50.

Quinta do Caracol

Tavira ☎281 322 475,
✉quintacaracol@netc.pt. Set in

lawned grounds north of the train station, this lovely farmhouse offers self-catering apartments sleeping 2–5 people in tastefully converted outbuildings. There are tennis courts, a tiny plunge pool, children's play area and bikes for rent. €150.

Vila Galé Albacora

☎281 380 800, ⊚www.vilagale.pt. A fascinating former tuna-fishing village (see p.86) has been tastefully converted into a four-star hotel. The best rooms face the river estuary, others face a car park or the enormous, flower-filled central courtyard. This also has a large pool, games room, restaurant and bar; inside there's another pool and health club. Courtesy public transport serves Tavira and the beach. The downside of its riverside position is a colony of voracious mosquitoes. €152, or €182 for river views.

Campsite

Camping Ilha de Tavira

☎281 321 709, ⊚www.campingtavira .com. Easter–Sept. Set under trees a minute from the sands and with a well-stocked mini market, this draws a youthful crowd. There's a kids' play area and ATM too, though it gets packed in July and August.

Cafés

Anazu

Rua Jacques Pessoa 11–13, Tavira
☎281 381 935. Daily 8am–midnight.
Lovely, tile-fronted riverfront café which catches the sun all day – a good place for breakfast or a sunset drink. There's a games-room/cybercafé attached.

Café Tavira Romana

Praça da República 24–26, Tavira
☎281 323 451. Daily 8am–midnight.
Great cakes and a huge variety of home-made ice creams make this a fine place to people watch, especially after 8pm or so when the cars in front of its street-side tables have dispersed.

Tavirense

Rua Marcelino Franco 19, Tavira. Daily 8am–midnight. Big, old-fashioned, *azulejo*-lined *pastelaria* opposite the cinema, serving great breakfasts, cakes and pastries.

Restaurants

Os Arcos

Rua João Vaz Corte Real 15, Tavira
☎281 324 392. Daily noon–10pm.
Good-value local serving fine, inexpensive grills, soups and salads. In summer, tables are placed in a superb riverfront position facing the old bridge. Full meals around €10.

▼RESTAURANTE BEIRA RIO

Beira Rio

Rua Borda da Àgua de Assêca 46–50, Tavira ☎281 323 165. Daily 6pm–midnight. Roomy riverside restaurant with arty pictures of Tavira on the walls and tree-shaded tables outdoors. Moderately priced international dishes include pizza, pasta, salads and vegetarian dishes; the inside bar area, complete with fishing boats for seats, is also worth sampling. Full meals around €15.

Bica

Rua Almirante Cândido dos Reis 22–24, Tavira ☎281 323 843. Daily noon–3pm & 7–10pm. Unglamorous but excellent-value meat, fish, *cataplanas* and omelettes, with plenty of locals and a TV for company. Main courses from around €5.

Capelo

Avda Eng. Duarte Pacheco, Santa Luzia ☎281 381 670. Mon–Tues & Thurs–Sun noon–2am. The nicest place to eat in Santa Luzia, with a spacious, *azulejo*-lined interior and an outdoor terrace. There's a long menu of well-prepared if slightly pricey fish and seafood.

João Belhi

Rua José Pires Padinha 96, Tavira ☎965 449 557. Daily noon–3pm & 4.30–10pm. Less expensive and more local than most of the restaurants on this stretch, with a menu featuring the usual fish and meat dishes and good house wine.

Kudissanga

Rua Dr. Augusta da Silva Carvalho 6, Tavira ☎281 321 670. Mon–Wed, Fri & Sun 7pm–2am, Sat noon–2pm & 7pm–2am. Excellent spot to sample decently priced cuisine from Portugal's former colonies. There is a good range of vegetarian food, as well as the speciality, boiled *mandioca* fish with *escabeche* or *mufete*, an Angolan dish of boiled beans with palm oil and grilled fish.

O Patio

Rua Dr. António Cabreira 30, Tavira ☎281 323 008 Mon–Sat noon–11.30pm. Pricey French-influenced restaurant with formal service and an attractive summer roof terrace. Specialities include lobster *cataplana*.

Pavilhão da Ilha

Ilha de Tavira ☎281 324 131. March–Oct daily noon–10pm. The best place on the island for a full meal, with tasty, moderately priced fish and grills and a lively bar area; it's just past the campsite as you head to the beach.

▼THE FERRY TO ILHA DE TAVIRA

Quatro Águas
Quatro Águas ☏281 325 329.
Tues–Sun noon–3pm & 7–10pm.
Highly rated seafood restaurant
specializing in dishes such as
açorda and *cataplana de marisco*
(seafood stews) and *bife de frango
com molho roquefort* (chicken with
Roquefort sauce).

Bars and clubs

Arco Bar
Rua Almirante Cândido dos Reis 67,
Tavira ☏918 504 200. Tues–Sun
10pm–2am. Unusually for the
Algarve, this is a gay-friendly
place attracting a laid-back
crowd; great for those into retro
and world music.

Patrick's
Rua Dr. António Cabreira 25–27, Tavira
☏281 325 998. Tues–Sat 6pm–1am.
Closed Nov. Welcoming *adega*-
style, English-run bar-restaurant
where, along with some familiar
beers, you can enjoy bar food
such as piri-piri prawns and
curries.

Ribeirinha
Mercado da Ribeira Loja 3, Tavira
☏965 384 464. Daily 9.30am–midnight; closed Thurs from Oct–May.
One of the best positioned of
the old market café-bars, a fine
spot for a beer or snack overlooking the river.

UBI
Rua Vale Caranguego, Tavira ☏281
322 555. July–Sept Tues–Sun midnight–6am; Oct–June Fri and Sat only.
On the eastern outskirts of town
– heading out via Rua Almirante Cândido dos Reis – Tavira's
only disco is housed in a huge,
metallic warehouse and plays a
mix of house, Latin and techno
grooves; the locals warm up with
a few pre-clubbing drinks in the
Bubi Bar in the same building
(open from 10pm).

The eastern Algarve

Though long popular with Spanish day-trippers, the eastern Algarve is only just being discovered as an alternative destination to the heavily developed central stretch. While Cabanas retains vestiges of its fishing village past, it is developing into a resort in its own right thanks to its excellent sandspit beach, the Praia de Cabanas. This spit can also be reached from Fábrica further east, near one of the prettiest villages in the Algarve, Cacela Velha. Beyond here, the sandspit begins to merge with the shoreline to give more accessible beaches at Manta Rota, Altura and Monte Gordo, the latter a lively resort and the last beach stop before the border.

Cabanas

With a kernel of atmospheric backstreets made up of colourful fishermen's houses, Cabanas consists largely of a line of fairly nondescript, low-rise shops, cafés and bars facing a picturesque river estuary. Moored fishing boats testify to the village's former mainstay, though nowadays the economy is largely driven by tourism thanks to the glorious sands on **Praia de Cabanas** over the estuary and the ruins of an old sea fort crumbling on the shoreline just east of town. Ferries shuttle passengers to the beach from a small jetty at the eastern edge of town (every 15min or so April–Oct; €1 return). Cross the dunes and you're faced with miles of golden sands, together with a couple of seasonal beach cafés.

▼CABANAS

Cacela Velha

Perched on a low cliff facing the estuary, the whitewashed village of Cacela Velha is a reminder of how the Algarve must have looked half a century ago. Apart from a couple of simple café-restaurants, there are no tourist facilities, just a pretty church and the remains of an eighteenth-century fort, and even that is a customs police station and closed to the public. Surrounded by olive groves, and offering exhilarating views from its clifftop, the village is highly picturesque, and despite the new golf courses just to the west it's rarely overrun by visitors.

To get here by public transport, you need to get the Tavira–Vila Real bus to set you down on the highway, just before Vila Nova de Cacela, from where it's a fifteen-minute walk down a signposted side road to the village.

The beach below the village, a continuation of **Praia de Cabanas**, is a beautiful, uncrowded long strand of soft sand backed by low dunes. To get to it by car, follow signs to Fábrica, just west of the village, around a kilometre downhill. There are a couple of restaurants next to the ferry (daily in summer but only during good weather the rest of the year; €1 return).

Manta Rota

Regular bus from Vila Real or Monte Gordo. Manta Rota is the first place east of Tavira where the beach is accessible by land. It's a superb, wide stretch of beach, although the village that backs it is a characterless splodge of villas and modern apartments. From Manta Rota you can walk along the beach all the way to the eastern edge of Portugal: from Manta Rota it's around thirty minutes to Alagoas, another twenty minutes to Praia Verde, and forty more on to Monte Gordo.

▼FILIGREE CHIMNEYS, CACELA VELHA

▲ THE BEACH AT MANTA ROTA

Altura

Altura is a large, modern and bustling resort spreading inland from another fine beach, Praia de Alagoas. The enormous sandy beach is well stocked with beach umbrellas, bars and water sports facilities, and though the town lacks much character, it's popular with Spanish and Portuguese holiday-makers which gives it a lively feel.

Praia Verde

Regular buses to Vila Real pass the side road to Praia Verde. Four kilometres along the main road from Altura, a wide expanse of wooded slopes give the name to the sands at **Praia Verde** (green beach). Despite the densely packed cubes that make up the holiday complex hidden in the trees, this remains the least-developed beach along this stretch, with just a couple of seasonal beach cafés and one restaurant. Further east, towards Monte Gordo, the beach becomes more unkempt, backed by scrubby dunes, but the sands are much less likely to be crowded in summer.

Monte Gordo

Monte Gordo ("fat mountain") is the last resort before the Spanish border and the most built-up of the eastern holiday towns. It's unashamedly high-rise, with new buildings still shooting up from the ground; even so, the plethora of Spanish day-trippers and big spenders lured by the seafront casino give the resort a buzz, while the beach, faced by a partly pedestrianized promenade, is wonderfully broad. A fleet of tractors keep the expanses clean at the end of each day, and there are even a few colourful fishing boats clustered round the western edge of town.

Walkers can head east up the beach to the mouth of the Rio Guadiana, from where you can stand at the most southwesterly

Visiting Monte Gordo

Buses from Vila Real and Tavira pull up close to the main Avenida Vasco de Gama at the seafront and adjacent to the casino. At the latter, there are plenty of car parking spaces. Just east of the casino is the turismo (☏ 281 544 495; May–Sept Tues–Thurs 9.30am–7pm; Fri–Mon 9.30am–1.30pm & 2.30–7pm; Oct–April Mon–Fri 10am–1.30pm & 2.30–6pm), which can hand out town maps and give details of private rooms.

point of Portugal and gaze over the border into Spain – about an hour's walk, past cocklers who dredge the sands at low tide.

Accommodation

Cantinho da Ria Formosa

Ribeira de Junco, Cacela Velha ☎281 951 837, ⓦwww.cantinhoriaformosa .com. Around 1km from the beach and the golf course, this blue-edged *residencial* sits in rural solitude on the road to Cacela Velha. Rooms are clean and modern, with views over the garden or fields. There are stables attached, and horse rides are on offer at around €15 an hour. €75.

Eurotel Altura

Altura ☎281 956 450, ⓦwww .eurotel-altura.co. A towering three-star hotel which dominates the beachfront. Views from the top floor rooms are stunning, and there are 135 large rooms. Rooms have disabled access and come with bath, TV and minibar; there's also an inside and outside pool, games room and tennis courts. €143.

Pensão Monte Gordo

Avda Infante Dom Henrique, Monte Gordo ☎281 542 124, ⓔpensa-montegordo@clix.pt. Set back from the main drag just west of the casino, this pleasant modern *pensão* offers large rooms with their own showers. €80.

Pedras da Rainha

Cabanas ☎281 380 680, ⓦwww .pedrasrainha@com. Well-run little resort with apartments and villas (sleeping up to ten) clustered around pleasant lawns, tennis courts and a large pool, all with disabled access. Two-bed apartments from €95.

Hotel Vasco da Gama

Avda Infante Dom Henrique, Monte Gordo ☎281 510 900, ⓦwww .hotelvascodagama.com. If you want to stay on the beach, then this decent high-rise is your best bet; some of the rooms have balconies, and there are also tennis courts, kids' play areas, a bar and restaurant. All rooms have TVs and en-suite bathrooms. €120, or rooms with sea-facing balconies €160.

Campsite

Parque de Campismo Municipal de Monte Gordo

Monte Gordo ☎281 510 970, ⓦwww .cm-vrsa.pt. This huge campsite is set under pines out on the Vila Real road, a short walk from the beach where there are plenty of

▼DOORWAY, MONTE GORDO

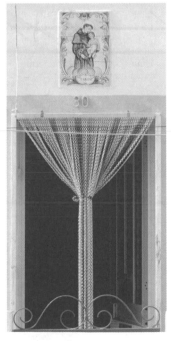

PLACES The eastern Algarve

▲PRAIA VERDE

inexpensive beach restaurants. The facilities are minimal, but the atmosphere is friendly and welcoming.

Cafés

Jaime
Monte Gordo ☎281 512 361.
Daily 9am–7pm. Simple beach café-restaurant facing the jumble of fishing boats west of the casino, a great spot for a light lunch or sunset beer.

Restaurants

Bate que eu Abre
Urbanizição Rota do Sul Lote E-1, Altura ☎281 956 656. Mon, Tues & Thurs–Sun 12.30–3pm & 7.30–11pm. A slightly formal, pricey but highly rated restaurant, tucked away in a residential part of Altura, though well signposted – its name means "knock and I'll open". The superbly prepared creations include meat fondue, *feijoada* and *bacalhau*.

O Costa
Fábrica, Cacela Velha ☎281 951 467. Daily noon–3pm & 7–11pm. Moderately priced fish and grilled

meats are served in an idyllic position on a broad terrace facing the waters.

O Firmo
Monte Gordo ☎281 513 280.
Daily noon–9pm. On the beach in front of the casino, this laid-back restaurant offers tasty grills and salads. It's not cheap, but the view from the terrace can't be faulted.

Das Mares
Praia de Alagoas, Altura ☎281 956 563. May–Sept Mon & Wed–Sun 10am–3pm & 7–11pm; Oct–April Mon & Wed–Sun 10am–3pm. The best of Altura's seafront café-restaurants, serving fine seafood, salads and omelettes right on the sands, at prices that won't burn a hole in your wallet.

Mota
Monte Gordo ☎281 512 340.
Daily 10am–10pm. Just east of the casino right on the sands, this is the best place to eat on the front, a big place specializing in *cataplanas*, *arroz* dishes, *feijoada* and moderately priced meat dishes.

Pedro
Rua Capitão Batista Marçal 51, Cabanas ☎281 370 425. Tues–Sun

12.30–3pm & 7.30–11pm. This attractive restaurant has a terrace facing the estuary. Grills are inexpensive, though the speciality *cataplanas* – including a delicious *cataplana de amêijoas* (with clams) – are more pricey.

Pezinhos

Praia Verde ☎281 513 195. Feb–Nov daily 10am–2am. Highly rated beachside restaurant serving expensive fish and seafood in a superb position right on the unspoilt sands.

Restinga

Manta Rota ☎281 951 388. April–Oct daily noon–10pm. Just back from Manta Rota's broad beach, this offers well-prepared and decently priced fish and Portuguese staples, in an attractive building just back from the beach with an outdoor terrace and well-used children's play area.

A Rocha

Avda 28 de Maio, Cabanas ☎281 370 239. Daily 12.30–3pm & 7–10pm. An attractive place with a breezy terrace where you can enjoy mid-priced omelettes, salads and fresh fish.

Bars

Quasimodo

Rua Capitão Jorge Ribeiro 1, Cabanas ☎281 370 559. Daily 8pm–2am. Popular bar specializing in loud music and cocktails, with "no coffee" as a warning that drinkers are the preferred clientele.

Vila Real, the Guadiana and the Serra de Alcaria

The broad Rio Guadiana marks the Algarve's eastern border with Spain. Until the 1990s, virtually the only route from the Algarve into Spain was to take a ferry from Vila Real, a historic border town which marks the end of the trans-Algarve railway line. The ferry remains the most fun way of visiting Spain, but nowadays a sleek suspension bridge whisks cars and buses straight over the permanently open border.

North of Vila Real, Castro Marim's historical role as a frontier town is still evident in its two spectacular forts, while further border fortifications are evident at the picturesque town of Alcoutim, forty kilometres to the north. The minor road hugging the river valley in between these two towns is a delight, while spectacular mountain scenery can be enjoyed inland from Alcoutim across the wild Serra de Alcaria, where virtually the only

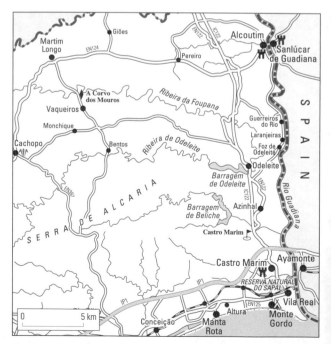

form of development is near Vaqueiros, with a mining village theme park, A Corvo dos Mouros.

Vila Real

The border town and harbour of Vila Real de Santo António has long been a favoured destination for Spanish day-trippers, lured by Portuguese food and cheap towels. And once past the modern suburbs, it's one of the more architecturally interesting towns on the Algarve. The original settlement was demolished by a tidal wave at the beginning of the seventeenth century, and the site stood empty until it was revived in 1774 by the Marquês de Pombal, the king's right-hand man. Eager to apply the latest concepts of town planning, Pombal used the same techniques he had already pioneered in Lisbon and rebuilt Vila Real on a grid plan.

The grid focuses on the handsome central square, Praça Marquês de Pombal, ringed by orange trees and low, white buildings, a couple of which are pleasant outdoor cafés.

Just north of the square, the **Centro Cultural António Aleixo** (Mon–Fri 10am–1pm & 3–7pm; free) on Rua Teófilo Braga, the old market building, has been reborn as an innovative space used for temporary exhibits and occasionally films. The centre also incorporates the Museu de Manuel Cabanas, displaying the works of a local painter and wood engraver.

The surrounding streets have a certain low-key charm, with rows of linen shops, electrical retailers and grocers. The riverside gardens are also attractive, with several cafés and fine views across the marina to Ayamonte in Spain.

▼PRAÇA MARQUÊS DE POMBAL, VILA REAL

PLACES Vila Real, the Guadiana and the Serra de Alcaria

Visiting Vila Real

Vila Real is the eastern terminal of the Algarve railway, and the station lies five minutes' walk north of the waterfront; turn left out of the station to get there. Buses (☏281 511 807) stop right on the riverfront itself or at the terminus just north of the train station. The turismo (Mon–Fri 10am–1.30pm & 2.30–6pm; ☏281 542 100) is situated in a corner of the old market building on Rua Teófilo Braga.

Train Station ▲   Ferry to Ayamonte (Spain) ▲

VILA REAL DE SANTO ANTÓNIO

RUA DE AYAMONTE

Bus Station

RUA DR. MANUEL ARRIAGA

RUA CÂNDIDO DOS REIS

RUA DR. SOUSA MARTINS

RUA A. CAPA

RUA JOSÉ BARÃO

RUA DA PRINCESA

AVENIDA DA REPÚBLICA

Rio Guadiana

Marina

N

RUA C.F. RAMIREZ

RUA TEÓFILO BRAGA

❶ ❼

Centro Cultural António Aleixo ❹

PR. MARQUES DE POMBAL

❸

RUA DOM PEDRO V

RUA 5 DE OUTUBRO

RUA DE MAIO

❽

RUA GENERAL HUMBERTO DELGADO

RUA DO BRAZIL

0   50 m

R. C. DA GRANDE GUERRA

❺

ACCOMMODATION	
Guadiana	A
Youth hostel	B

EATING & DRINKING	
Os Arcos	5
Arenilha	4
Cantinho do Marquês	2
Caves do Guadiana	3
O Coração da Cidade	1

Into Spain: Ayamonte

A fun half-day's excursion is to take the ferry from Vila Real over to Ayamonte in Spain (every 40mins from 8.40am, last return 7pm, which is 8pm Spanish time; €1.10 single). The crossing takes twenty minutes, and is a lovely ride across the Guadiana with the forts of Castro Marim visible to the west and the impressive bridge to the north.

Ferries stop at Ayamonte's dull waterfront, but when you head 200m or so inland to Plaza de la Laguna you'll quickly realize

you are in Spain: it's a delightful palm-lined square with bright, Moorish-influenced tiled benches. Just south of the square is the town's handsome church, Parroquia de las Angustias, around which is a warren of characterful backstreets, the shops seeming spruce and upmarket in comparison with Vila Real.

South of the church is another square, the long palm-fringed Plaza de la Ribeira, adjacent to some small docks and surrounded by inexpensive cafés and tapas bars.

▼THIS WAY TO SPAIN, VILA REAL

Visiting Castro Marim

Buses to Castro Marim from Vila Real (several daily Mon–Fri, two at weekends) pull up near the tourist office on the main Rua de São Sebastião. The turismo is on Rua José Alves Moreira 2–4, next to a tiny square, Praça 1º de Maio (Mon–Fri 10am–1.30pm & 2.30–6pm; ☎281 531 232), just below the castle, with an attractive café.

Castro Marim and around

The village of Castro Marim was once a key fortification protecting Portugal's southern coast. Nowadays it's a sleepy place that only comes alive in late August when it holds the **Medieval Days festival**, with jousting, lute players and craft stalls. The festival commemorates the fact that Castro Marim was the first headquarters for the Order of Christ, who were based at a huge **castle** (daily: April–Oct 9am–7pm; Nov–March 9am–5pm; free), built by Afonso III in the thirteenth century and rebuilt during the War of Restoration in 1640. The little chapel inside the castle was regularly visited by Henry the Navigator. Most of the castle was destroyed in the Great Earthquake of 1755, with only the gate and outer walls surviving. You can clamber up the walls for fine views across the mud flats of the Reserva Natural do Sapal and the impressive modern suspension bridge to Spain. A small **museum** inside the castle walls (free) displays local archaeological, ethnographical and geographical exhibits, including ceramics and carpets.

Further fine views are to be had from the smaller thirteenth-century Fortaleza de São Sebastião, whose ruins cap the hilltop opposite.

Reserva Natural do Sapal

The Reserva Natural do Sapal is a wide, flat area of marshland that spreads around Castro Marim and forms the habitat for some important and unusual wildlife. The turismo in Castro Marim can give out maps with walking routes through the reserve and direct you to the remote reserve headquarters (Mon–Fri 9am–12.30pm

▼CASTRO MARIM

▲RESERVA NATURAL DO SAPAL

& 2–5.30pm; ☎281 510 680). One of the area's most unusual and elusive inhabitants is the extraordinary, ten-centimetre-long, swivel-eyed, Mediterranean chameleon. Though common in North Africa, it is only found in Europe here and in isolated spots in Spain and Crete.

Odeleite and Foz de Odeleite

North of Castro Marim, once clear of the IP1 to Spain and the new golf course, the fast EN122 heads into the least-visited part of the Algarve. There are some good picnic spots at a couple of attractive **reservoirs** (barragens) signposted off the road at Beliche and Odeleite, but the most scenic route is along the side road signed to Foz de Odeleite and Alcoutim. Infrequent buses from Vila Real follow the EN122 on school days only, calling at the tiny village of Foz de Odeleite and at Alcoutim.

Foz de Odeleite is an attractive village at the mouth (*foz*) of the Rio Odeleite, a tributary of the Guadiana. Boat trips often stop off here while groups are taken round to see the communal bread ovens and traditional flat roofs of the village, used to dry pumpkins and fruits during the summer months. There are four good marked walks either side of the village; the best is an eleven-kilometre/two-hour return trip to the village of Odeleite, signposted along the Rio Odeleite. Alternatively, it's around 15km from Foz de Odeleite to Alcoutim along the Guadiana, a river which Nobel prize for literature winner José Saramago says "was born beautiful and will end its days beautiful: such is its destiny".

Gueirreiros do Rio and along the Guadiana

Gueirreiros do Rio is a small, traditional village on the banks of the wide Guadiana, its fertile shores planted with citrus and almond trees that

Guadiana boat trips

Various companies offer day cruises up the Guadiana, departing from Vila Real harbour. Some go as far as Alcoutim (see p.103), around 40km away, others to Foz de Odeleite, around half that distance. Either trip is idyllic, passing through unspoilt, rolling countryside dotted with olive groves, with the opportunity for swimming stops. Prices start at around €50 per person, which includes lunch. Turismar (☎281 956 634/968 831 553) are a good first port of call.

blossom. It's worth a brief stopover for its tiny **Museu do Rio** (℡281 547 380; Tues–Sat: May–Sept 2–5.30pm; Oct–April 9am–12.30pm & 1.30–5pm; €2.50), one of the region's several Núcleos Museológicos (see p.104). Set in one room of a former primary school, the museum consists of sketches, maps, photos and factsheets related to the river's wildlife and history; all the labels are in Portuguese. The village café (Mon & Wed–Sun 9.30am–8pm) is along the little backstreet opposite the museum.

Alcoutim

The picturesque village of Alcoutim has a long history as a river port, dominated in turn by Greeks, Romans and Moors who, over the centuries, fortified its riverside hilltop with various structures to protect the copper transported down river from the nearby mines at São Domingos. Nowadays Alcoutim survives largely on tourists attracted by its tranquil riverside position and the fourteenth-century hilltop **castle** (℡281 546 511; daily 9am–1pm & 2–5pm;

€2.50), a leafy ruin filled with trees and offering fine views over the town and into Spain. The entrance fee includes access to a small **archaeological museum** by the main gates, which traces the history of the castle, its active service in the War of Restoration and the Liberal Wars, and the remnants of earlier structures on the site. The same ticket gives access to a rather dull sacred art collection in the nearby Ermida de Nossa Senhora de Conceição, together with other museums in the region (see p.104).

From the castle, cobbled backstreets lead down to the small main square, below which lies the appealing riverfront. The river currents are too strong for safe swimming, but off the Mertola road on the edge of town is a small river beach (*praia fluvial*). A few huts front a little bathing area on the banks of the Rio Cadavais – a popular summer spot for picnics.

Into Spain: Sanlúcar

From Alcoutim waterfront, a **ferry** (daily 9am–1pm & 2–7pm; €1 single) heads over the

▼ALCOUTIM

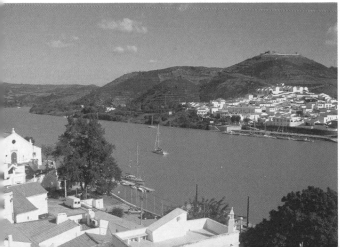

Visiting Alcoutim

Buses pull in adjacent to the small main square, Praça da República, near the turismo (Mon–Fri: May–Oct 10am–1.30pm & 2.30–7pm; Nov–April same hours until 6pm; ☎281 546 179).

Guadiana to the Spanish village of **Sanlúcar**, a mirror image of Alcoutim, with its own ruined castle and lovely views back over Portugal. Although euros are now the shared currency, the clocks are still an hour apart, usually chiming slightly out of sync. There's a little café right by the ferry terminal on the other side if you fancy a *café con leche*.

Núcleos Museológicos

The Núcleos Museológicos is a collective of small museums set up in otherwise neglected agri-cultural villages in an attempt to lure visitors out of their cars into the remote but beautiful region around Alcoutim. It's a worthy concept, though none of the museums warrants more than a ten-minute leg stretch. A ticket for €2.50 allows entry to any of the participating museums. Apart from the museum in Alcoutim (see p.103), the museums open on a rotation basis. Check with the turismo in Alcoutim for the latest times, or call ☎281 540 509.

The first museum stop – though it's not much cop unless you understand Portu-guese – can be made at the tiny village of **Pereiro**, where the museum of popular culture (☎281 547 184) displays poems, superstitions and local customs. Another 8km west, a signed road right to Giões takes you to a tiny agricultural hamlet with its own artisans' museum (☎281 547 474), a diminutive space displaying rugs, carpets, ceramics and the like. At **Santa Justa**'s

museum (☎281 498 677), the former primary school has been set out as it would have looked in the 1950s and makes for one of the more engaging stops. At the otherwise dull village of **Martim Longo**, a history museum (☎281 498 682) dis-plays an eclectic collection of maps, agricultural implements, lamps, rugs and old radios. See opposite for details of Vaqueiros.

A Corvo dos Mouros

☎281 498 505, ⊛www .minacovamouros.sitepac.pt. Daily: March–May & Nov 10.30am–4.30pm; June–Oct 10.30am–6pm. €7.50, under-10s €5. A Corvo dos Mouros is an innovative, German-run theme park built on the site of an ancient gold and copper mine. Discovered in 1865, the mines date back to around 2500 BC. Stone moulds, primitive furnaces for smelt-ing ore, copper axes, chisels and saws, rock tombs and two Roman villas have all been dis-covered at the site. Subsequently abandoned, the site was bought up in the 1990s and today consists of a replica furnace, reconstructed thatched medi-eval houses typical of the Serra do Caldeirão, and slightly eery dummies posing as Stone Age figures. The site is all described by an English audio guide and linked by a 1km trail which passes old mine shafts and wells. There are also donkey rides for kids (€6–8 extra) and a café. You can walk down to natural pools where you can have a dip in the Rio Foupana.

The site also acts as a reserve for native wildlife; if you're lucky you can spot deer and rare griffin vultures, and there is also a bird recovery centre.

Vaqueiros and around

The village of Vaqueiros – its church crowned with a giant stork's nest – contains the last of the region's Núcleo Museológicos (see opposite, ☎281 498 511), an agricultural museum dedicated to man's relationship with nature and family life in a rural village; exhibits include olive presses, old measures, pots and pans.

There are two great drives from Vaqueiros. Turn left at Montinho da Revelada and via the tiny hamlet of Monchique and the road begins to cross a high pass with stunning views over the Serra de Alcaria. The road eventually snakes down to join the EN397 linking Tavira to Cachopo. Alternatively continue straight on towards Bentos and follow signs to Tavira, the road snaking through wild scenery and remote agricultural villages, over the Ribeira de Odeleite.

Accommodation

Afonso

Rua Dr. João Dias 10, Alcoutim ☎281 546 211. Just uphill from the main square, this small but spruce modern *pensão* offers pleasant rooms with their own baths, though the price does not include breakfast. €30.

Estalagem do Guadiana

Alcoutim ☎281 540 120, ☻www .grupofbarata.com. Much the smartest place in Alcoutim – head north out of Alcoutim and follow the signs. A swish modern inn with its own pool, tennis court, restaurant (daily noon–3pm & 7–10pm) and Saturday night entertainment. Spacious rooms come with satellite TV, baths and fine river views. €85.

Hotel Guadiana

Avda da Republica, Vila Real ☎281 511 482, ☻www.hotelguadiana.com .pt. A national monument, with a grand exterior and fine Art Deco touches, including a fine dining room. Characterful, but despite the TVs and en-suite bathrooms, the high-ceilinged rooms are showing their age. €70.

Youth hostel (Alcoutim)

Alcoutim ☎ & ☎281 546 004 ☻www .pousadasjuventude.pt The very smart fifty-bed youth hostel is around 1.5km north of the village, across the Ribeira Cadavais; cross the bridge beyond Praça da República and follow the signs. It has its own canteen, bar and launderette as well as disabled access, and can help with canoe and bike rental. Double rooms from €37; four-bed dorms from €14.

Youth hostel (Vila Real)

Rua Dr. Sousa Martins 40, Vila Real ☎ & ☎281 544 565, ☻www .pousadasjuventude.pt. Recently renovated, the town youth hostel is a characterful if cramped place set in an old town house. The pleasant communal areas include a bar, and there are a handful of doubles and twins (from €20) and various dorms of three, four or six beds (from €10).

Cafés and bars

Café Cantinho de Marquês

Praça Marquês de Pombal 24, Vila Real ☎281 544 483. Mon–Sat 8am–11pm. Busy café with tables spilling out onto the main square under fragrant orange trees. The perfect drink stop, and it also does a mean *rissóis de bacalhau*.

O Coração da Cidade

Rua Dr. Teófilo Braga, Vila Real ☎281 543 303.Daily 7.30am–10pm. On the corner of Rua Almirante Cândido dos Reis, just north of the market building, this all-purpose café-restaurant sells everything from snacks and drinks to full meals. Always lively downstairs, though the upstairs restaurant can be too quiet.

Passage Café

Plaza de la Laguna 11, Ayamonte ☎959 470 978. Mon–Sat 8am–4.30pm, Sun noon–4.30pm. Jazzy, wood-panelled café-bar serving cakes and snacks; outdoor tables front the picturesque main square.

O Soeiro

Rua Município, Alcoutim ☎281 546 241. Café Mon–Sat 9am–11pm; restaurant Mon–Fri noon–3pm.With outdoor tables on a little terrace right above the waterfront, this is a lovely spot for a drink or snack, with inexpensive lunchtime grills cooked on an outside barbecue in summer.The upstairs restaurant (lunches only) does a good range of moderately priced meals, including game and river fish such as *lampreia* (lamprey), the local specialities.

Restaurants

Alcatia

Rua de Timor 8970, Alcoutim ☎281 546 606. Tues–Sun noon–3pm & 7–10pm. Despite its unpromising location in a shopping centre on the way to the youth hostel, about 1km out of town, this modern restaurant offers fine local cuisine including wild boar, rabbit and hare at very reasonable prices.

Os Arcos

Avda da República 45, Vila Real ☎281 543 764. Daily 12.30–3pm & 7.30–11pm. Bustling neighbourhood restaurant serving a good range of inexpensive Portuguese nosh, including some good rice dishes. It also has an attached *pastelaria*.

Restaurante Caves do Guadiana

Avda da República 89–90, Vila Real ☎281 544 498. Mon–Wed & Fri–Sun noon–3pm & 7–10pm. The best place in town for a quality meal at moderate prices. It's got a nice tiled, vaulted interior and offers a long list of fish, grilled meats and omelettes.

Churrasqueira Arenilha

Rua Cândido dos Reis, Vila Real ☎281 544 038. Daily noon–3pm & 7–11pm. Opposite the market building, the attractive interior is lined with old black-and-white photos of Vila Real. The Portuguese food is nothing special but prices are low and the atmosphere animated.

Eira Gaio

Rua 25 de Abril, Castro Marim ☎281 351 358. Mon–Sat noon–3pm & 7–10pm, Sun noon–3pm. On the road opposite the tourist office, this simple local diner has a limited but inexpensive menu with good *bacalhau* dishes.

Albufeira and around

Albufeira has long been the most popular resort in the Algarve. Its name derives from the Moorish occupation when it was called "Al-buhera", Castle of the Sea, and sat on a low clifftop overlooking a stunning beach. The historic centre is a picturesque medley of dazzling whitewashed churches and terracotta-roofed houses. Around the old centre lies an enormous swathe of development, but at least the villas, hotels, bars and restaurants that radiate for miles outwards are largely

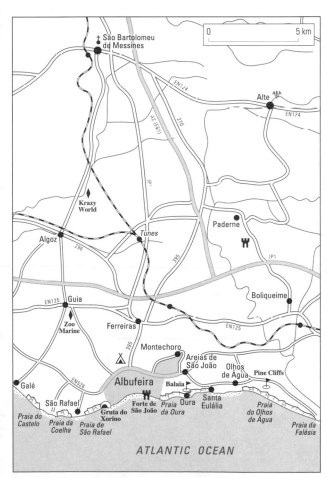

lowrise and invisible from the beach itself. If you miss your home comforts, you'll find bars that pull in punters with live cricket or British soccer on TV, and you're never far away from a café offering a full English breakfast.

Within the vicinity, there are fine walks round the historic castle at Paderne, while Alte, set in the foothills of the Serra de Caldeirão, is one of the Algarve's prettiest and best-kept villages.

Around Largo Engenheiro Duarte Pacheco

The focus of historic Albufeira is the **main square**, Largo Engenheiro Duarte Pacheco, a pretty pedestrianized space with a small fountain and benches beneath palms trees. But, although the surrounding buildings are traditionally Portuguese, their contents are decidedly international, mostly pizza restaurants and bars with English names. After dark, the square becomes a focus for families and promenaders, accompanied in high season by live performers and buskers.

Off the square, **Rua Candida dos Reis** permanently buzzes, by day with little craft stalls and after dark with row upon row of bars selling cheap cocktails. The south side of the square contains the Galeria de arte Pintor Samora Barros (July to mid-Sept daily 5.30–11pm; mid-Sept to end of June Mon–Sat 10.30am–5pm; free), an art gallery named after contemporary local artist Samora Barros, who specializes in relief paintings of Portuguese themes. South of the square, Rua 5 de Outubro leads to the dramatic tunnel that has been blasted through the cliff to give access to the beach.

Praça Miguel Bombarda

Praça Miguel Bombarda is a small square close to two of the town's most important churches. On the square itself, the **Ermide de São Sebastião** has a distinctive Manueline door, though most of the building was constructed in the early eighteenth century with

▼NIGHTTIME IN LARGO ENGENHEIRO DUARTE PACHECO

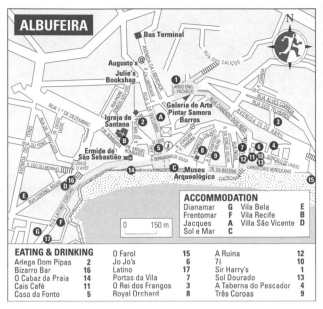

ALBUFEIRA

Bus Terminal

Augusto's @

Julie's Bookshop

Galeria de Arte Pintar Samora Barros

Igreja de Santana

Ermide de São Sebastião

Museu Arqueológico

ACCOMMODATION			
Dianamar	**G**	Vila Bela	**E**
Frentomar	**F**	Vila Recife	**B**
Jacques	**A**	Villa São Vicente	**D**
Sol e Mar	**C**		

0   150 m

EATING & DRINKING					
Adega Dom Pipas	2	O Farol	15	A Ruina	12
Bizarro Bar	16	Jo Jo's	6	7½	10
O Cabaz da Praia	14	Latino	17	Sir Harry's	1
Cais Café	11	Portas da Vila	7	Sol Dourado	13
Casa da Fonte	5	O Rei dos Frangos	3	A Taberna do Pescador	4
		Royal Orchard	8	Três Coroas	9

Baroque touches. Today the hermitage contains the **Museu Arte Sacra** (July–Oct 10am–midnight; free), a diminutive sacred-art museum containing plaster images of saints.

Igreja de Santana

Just north of the museum is the **Igreja de Santana**, a white-washed eighteenth-century church with an attractive dome.

From the patio at the front there are lovely views over the distinctive filigree chimneys of the old town to the sea.

Museu Arqueológico

Travessa da Bateria ☎289 588 798. Tues–Sun: mid-Sept to May 10am–5pm; June to mid-Sept 2.30–8pm. Free. Albufeira's most interesting museum, the Museu Arqueológico, is in the former

---

Visiting Albufeira

Albufeira's bus terminal (☎289 589 755) is on Avenida da Liberdade, five minutes' walk from the central square, Largo Engenheiro Duarte Pacheco. Albufeira's nearest train station is actually 6km north of town at Ferreiras; a bus connects it with the bus terminal every 45 minutes or so (daily 7am–8pm), or a taxi will set you back about €8, depending on the time of day. There's a large, free car park a block back from the bus station; any closer in and you have to pay to park, though there are usually free places to the west of town – follow signs to "Albufeira Ponte".

The turismo (☎289 585 279; Oct–May Mon & Fri–Sat 9.30am–12.30pm & 1.30–5.30pm, Tues–Thurs 9.30am–5.30pm; June–Sept same hours until 7pm) is on Rua 5 de Outubro, close to the tunnel.

town hall. It has a rather sparse but well laid-out collection of artefacts gathered from the area dating from Neolithic times to the present. There are fragments of mosaics from a Roman villa unearthed nearby, Visigoth rock tombs and jars, and even a Moorish silo excavated in situ beneath the museum. More recent remains include Manueline fragments from the old Igreja Matriz, while upstairs there are atmospheric black-and-white photos showing the town and its beach with barely a trace of tourism.

Travessa da Bateria

Beyond the museum, Travessa da Bateria runs parallel to the beach past some of the town's most atmospheric backstreets – Rua do Cemitério Velho, Rua da Igreja Velha and Rua Nova – narrow cobbled streets lined with little cottages. At the

▼OLD TOWN STREETS

end of Travessa da Bateria, steps wind down to the beach via the former fish market, which is now a shelter for buskers and people chilling out under its shady roof.

Albufeira beach

The beach fronting Albufeira is a glorious sweep of soft sand flanked by strange tooth-like rock formations and backed by a sandstone cliff. The western end of the beach can be reached via the tunnel or via steep steps which wind down the cliff below the *Hotel Rocamar*. This tends to be the busiest stretch of sand, where you can hire out pedaloes or be whisked out water-skiing or on inflatable bananas.

Where this section of the beach ends, a path continues round the headland, before winding up to join Rua Latino Coelho high above a brand-new yachting marina backed by an alarming Legoland conglomeration of brightly coloured modern houses. En route you pass a grotto, Gruta do Xorino, which was used as a hideout by liberals during the Miguelite wars in 1833; today it's the haunt of local kids who swim in the shimmering green waters.

The eastern end of the beach is divided by a concrete jetty next to the fisherman's beach. When the waves get up, this is the most popular section for surfers.

At low tide you can walk on for another twenty minutes or so beyond the jetty below more low cliffs. The sand here is marginally less busy, though still backed by the odd beach café. Take care when swimming as the beach becomes gradually rockier towards the cliffs at the far end. You can clamber on to

▲ALBUFEIRA TOWN BEACH

the low cliffs beyond here and follow the coastal paths round to Praia da Oura, a 15 minute walk passing a series of natural grottoes, rock bridges and blowholes carved into the rock by the sea.

Montechoro

Much of Albufeira's package accommodation is slightly away from the historic centre, in one of the handful of small resort-villages on either side. The largest of these, Montechoro, is a downmarket suburb known as "the strip" with a gaudy Eurotrashy appeal. A toy train circles Albufeira out to Montechoro every twenty minutes or so from 9.20am–midnight (€2 a trip, or €3/6 a half/full-day pass).

Nearby, east of the centre, lies Albufeira's bullring. The tourist office can give details of the weekly May-to-October **bull-fights**.

Beaches west of Albufeira

Ongoing building may soon change things, but for now the stunning cove beaches that begin a couple of kilometres to the west of Albufeira are less developed than those to the east; this is where Cliff Richard chose to build his summer villa. The first of the beaches, **São Rafael**, is a lovely Blue Flag sandy cove studded with sandstone pillars and backed by low cliffs, with its own swanky restaurant.

Also with a beach café-restaurant, and reached down a steep road, Praia do Castelo is a smaller sandy bay nestling below cliffs. Usually the quietest beach on this stretch is **Praia da Coelho**, reached down a delightful sandy track through unspoilt countryside, around a ten-minute walk from the car park. Development becomes more intense at **Praia de Galé**, where the massive sweeping swathe of sand stretches all the way west to Armação de Pêra (see p.119). Another Blue Flag beach with a cluster of hotels, cafés and restaurants, this is as good a place as any to enjoy a day on the beach.

Krazy World

☎282 574 134, ⊛www.krazy-world
.com. Jan–April & Oct–Dec Wed–Sun
10am–5.30pm; May–Sept daily
10am–7.30pm. €17, under-12s €10;
family ticket €40. Buses from Albufeira
to São Bartolomeu de Messines stop
near the entrance. Around eighteen kilometres northwest of
Albufeira is a sizeable zoo-cum-
theme park, Krazy World. The
entrance fee includes the neatly
landscaped park, fairground
– mostly traditional rides such as
ferris wheels and roundabouts –
as well as a mini zoo, children's
farm, swimming pools and crazy
golf course. Quad bikes and
bumper cars cost extra, and in
high season expect to queue for
the more popular rides.

Paderne

Served by hourly buses from Albufeira.
The main appeal of Paderne,
a traditional village set on a
low hill, lies in strolling round
the sloping streets and soaking
up the relaxed atmosphere. Its
only real sight is the parish
church, which dates from 1506
– its doorway retains some
fine Manueline flourishes. A
worthy detour is the pleasant
walk to the scant remains of

a **Moorish castle**, which lie
some 2km southeast of town
on the road to Boliqueime.
The castle is signed down a
dirt track, officially labelled as a
1.4km pedestrian route, though
a steady stream of cars usually
bumps its way up the track to
avoid the steep final ascent.
Nearby motorway aside, it's a
lovely walk through olive groves,
accompanied by the rhythmic
screech of cicadas.

At the top of the hill lie
the atmospheric remains of a
twelfth-century Moorish fort
which commands great views
of the surrounding countryside. The fort was captured
by knights from the Order
of Christ in 1248 during the
Christian reconquest of the
Algarve, and you can still see
remains of the later brick
fourteenth-century hermitage,
the Ermida de Nossa Senhora
do Castelo, inside the castle's
crumbly walls.

São Bartolomeu de Messines

Served by regular buses from Albufeira, Portimão and Silves. The
small, unspoilt market town of
São Bartolomeu de Messines
preserves an important six-

▼KRAZY WORLD

▲PADERNE CASTLE

teenth-century parish **church**, remodelled in Baroque style and incorporating Manueline interior columns decorated with twisted stone rope. Nowadays, the only time the town is remotely animated is on the last Monday of the month, when it hosts a livestock market just off the central Rua 1 Maio.

Alte

Tumbling down a hillside, a series of narrow cobbled streets make Alte one of the region's most picturesque villages, an asset well exploited by tour operators who ship in day-trippers throughout the summer. Come early or at the end of the day, however, and the place is given over to locals once more.

Alte's only sight is the graceful sixteenth-century Igreja Matriz, with a Manueline doorway, though most people spend their time wandering round the cobbled backstreets and out to a couple of natural springs or *fontes* around ten minutes' walk from the centre. The first of these, Fonte Pequena, is marked by the restaurant of the same name set in an old mill. A further five

minutes' walk up a reed-filled valley lies the larger and more appealing Fonte Grande, where the river passes an old weir lined with picnic tables set under shady trees.

Alte also holds a lively flea market on the third Thursday of every month.

▼ALTE

Visiting Alte

Alte is poorly served by public transport, with just one bus daily from Loulé, though it is well served by summer tours and jeep safaris; ask around at the travel agents in Albufeira for details.

The turismo is located on the main road just below town on the Estrada da Ponte (Mon 9am–12.30pm & 2–5.30pm, Tues–Fri 9am–5.30pm, Sat 9.30am–11.30pm & 2–4.30pm; ☎289 478 666).

Guia

Guia is a typical inland Algarve town with a couple of historic churches, the seventeenth-century Igreja Matriz and the Baroque Nossa Senhora da Guia. The latter has a particularly striking interior of sumptuous blue and white *azulejos*. The town is also famed for its chicken restaurants, several specialising in delicious chargrilled *frango*.

Zoo Marine

☎289 560 300, ⊛www.zoomarine .com. May to June 22 & Sept 19 to end Oct daily 10am–5pm; June 23– Sept 18 daily 10am–8pm; Nov to April Tues–Sun 10am–5pm. Adults €19, children €11.50. Right on the main EN125, this part-zoo and part-theme park boasts swimming pools, fairground rides, an aquarium and animal enclosures. Various shows are staggered throughout the day, including performing parrots, sea lion performances and a spectacular dolphin show. With inexpensive cafés into the bargain, Zoo Marine can make a pretty perfect family day out.

Accommodation

Alte Hotel

Moninho, near Alte ☎289 478 523, ⊛www.altehotel.com. This modern hotel is on a rural hillside some 1km out of Alte, with its own restaurant, pool and superb views from most of the comfortable en-suite rooms. €84.

Pensão Dianamar

Rua Latino Coelho 36, Albufeira ☎289 587 801, ⊛www.dianamar.com. Well-run Swedish-owned *pensão* in the nicest part of town, a block back from the beach. The simple en-suite rooms are spotless and those at the top have great sea views, as does the communal roof terrace. A superb Swedish breakfast including yoghurts, fruit and cakes costs extra.

Pensão Residencial Frentomar

Rua Latino Coelho, Albufeira ☎289 512005, ⊛frentomar@sapo.pt. Simple, clean rooms on a quiet side road just above the steps down to the beach. Try to get one with a terrace and a sea view, though these are usually snapped up quickly. €50.

Jacques Accommodation

Rua 5 de Outubro 36, Albufeira ☎969 584 933. Set in an attractive town house on the main pedestrianized street, this offers large, airy en-suite rooms, some with balconies, although front rooms can be noisy. There's a shared terrace, and each floor has an area with a fridge and coffee-making facilities. Breakfast not included. April–Oct. €50.

Hotel Sol e Mar

Rua Bernardino de Sousa, Albufeira ☎289 580 080, ⊛grupofbarata.co.

On the cliff above the tunnel to the beach, this characterless but well-equipped four-star stretches down five floors right onto the beach. The balconies have a prime spot overlooking the sands, while there's also a swimming pool. Rates drop considerably out of season. €120.

Residencial Vila Bela

Rua Coronel Águas 32, Albufeira ☎ & ☎289 512 101, ✉ctr@mal.telepac .pt. A good-value *residencial* with rooms overlooking a small swimming pool; top ones have balconies with fine sea views. There is a pleasant patio brightened by bougainvillea. Often booked up by tour groups. April–Oct. €60.

Estalagem Vila Joya

Praia da Galé ☎289 591 795, ⊛www .vilajoya.de. One of the Algarve's most exclusive "gourmet" hotels, with a renowned two Michelin-star restaurant downstairs (featuring an a la carte lunch menu and evening menu *degustacion*). The pseudo-Moorish hotel has its own pool sitting right above the beach. There are just twelve luxurious rooms and five suites. €400. Closed Nov–March.

Residencial Vila Recife

Rua Miguel Bombarda 6, Albufeira ☎289 583 740, ✉vila.recife@iol .pt. A huge, rambling old town house complete with its own garden and small pool. The rooms are smallish but comfortable with en-suite facilities, some with seaviews, and the *azulejos*-lined communal areas are spotless. The garden bar, complete with ceiling fans and snooker table, has live music most nights. €80.

Villa São Vicente Hotel

Largo Jacinto D'Ayet 4, Albufeira ☎289 583 700, ⊛hotel-vila-sai-vicente.com. A tasteful modern three-star with tiled floors and white-washed walls. It has its own small pool and a terrace facing the beach. Rooms facing the street are cheaper, but it's worth paying extra for sea views. All rooms are en suite with TVs and a/c. €110–130.

Campsite

Parque de Campismo

Estrada de Ferreiras, Albufeira ☎289 587 629, ✉campingalbufeira@mail .telepac.pt. The finely appointed (and expensive) local campsite, complete with swimming pools, restaurants, bars, shops and tennis courts – is 2km to the north of town, off the N396, with regular bus connections to town (any bus to Ferreiras passes it), though space can be at a premium in high season – book ahead if possible.

Shops

Julie's Bookshop

Rua Igreja Nova 6, Albufeira. Mon–Fri 10am–6pm, Sat 10am–1pm, Sun 10am–3pm. Well-stocked little shop stocking a large range of English and foreign-language books geared towards beach reading.

Albufeira Gypsy market

Caliços (north of the centre). 1st & 3rd Tues of each month, 9am–1pm. Lively flea market, a good place to pick up inexpensive clothes and ceramics. A smaller, daily clothes market sets up by the bus terminal on Avenida da Liberdade.

PLACES Albufeira and around

Cafés

Cais Café

Cais Herculano, Albufeira ☎289 512 719. Daily 8am–midnight. Aromatic café offering a fine selection of tempting pastries and refreshing homemade ice creams.

Sol Dourado

Cais Herculano, Albufeira. Daily 9.30am–9pm. Relatively inexpensive (for this part of town) breakfasts, sandwiches, milkshakes and Portuguese dishes are served on a breezy roof terrace overlooking the fishing boats right on the beach.

Restaurants

Adega Dom Pipas

Trav dos Arcos 78, Albufeira ☎289 588 091. Daily 11am–3pm & 6.30pm–midnight. The mock olde-worlde decor and moderate Portuguese staples are nothing special, but this restaurant does have outdoor tables on what it claims is "the most typical street in Albufeira", an attractive narrow alley usually strung over with coloured ribbons for shade.

Bar Pic Nic

Praia do Castelo ☎289 591 844. Daily 10am–11pm, closed Nov–Feb. Superb beachside café-restaurant wedged into cliffs behind the sands. Prices are moderate, with great grilled meats, though as you'd expect, fresh fish is the best bet.

O Cabaz da Praia

Praça Miguel Bombarda 7, Albufeira ☎289 512 137. Daily noon–2pm & 7–10pm. With a roof terrace offering fine views over the beach, this French-inspired restaurant serves excellent but expensive meals (€20 and upwards). Dishes include duck breast with quince and honey, onion soup, carpaccio of salmon and a long list of desserts.

Casa da Fonte

Rua João de Deus 7, Albufeira ☎289 514 578. Daily noon–3pm & 7pm–midnight. This popular restaurant is set round a beautiful Moorish-style courtyard complete with *azulejos*, lemon trees and a resident parrot. The extensive menu features the usual range of mid-priced fish and meats, but arrive early as the courtyard tables fill up fast.

Restaurante O Farol

Praia dos Pescadores, Albufeira ☎289 513 552. Daily 10am–11pm. Simple beachside café-restaurant right behind the boats on the fisherman's beach. The generous portions of fresh fish and grilled meats are good value, and the atmosphere is refreshingly unpretentious – though service can be excessively laid-back.

Restaurante Fonte Pequena

Fonte Pequena, Alte ☎289 478 509. Tues–Sun: April–Sept noon–3pm & 7–10pm; Oct–March 9.30am–5pm. A large rustic-style grill house with wooden benches laid out on a shady terrace facing the water at the *fonte*. Throughout the year there's live folk music on Wednesdays. Around €15 for a full meal.

O Rei dos Frangos

Trav dos Telheiros 4, off Avda 25 de Abril, Albufeira ☎289 512 981. Daily noon–3.30pm & 6pm–midnight. A first-rate little *churrasqueria* – the chicken comes smothered in piri-piri and there's also grilled steak, swordfish and a speciality meat *cataplana*. Unglamorous but good value.

Royal Orchard

Beco Bernardino de Sousa, Albufeira
☏ 289 502 505. Daily 12.30–2.30pm
& 7.30–11pm. Next to the
archaeological museum, this
moderately priced Thai
restaurant has sumptuous Thai
decor and tables laid out in a
superb leafy courtyard. The long
menu features noodle and rice
dishes with fish, meat or seafood,
plus vegetarian options.

A Taberna do Pescador

Trav Cais Herculano, Albufeira ☏ 289
589 196. Daily noon–3pm & 6–11pm.
A rarity in central Albufeira: an
authentic Portuguese *taberna*
attracting as many locals as
tourists. The well-priced fish,
seafood and meats (main
courses around €10) are grilled
to perfection on an outdoor
terrace, and portions are huge;
wash it all down with the house
sangria.

A Ruina

Largo Cais Herculano, Albufeira ☏ 289
512 094. Daily 12.30–3pm & 7–11pm.
Large, high-profile restaurant set
in the cliffs behind the beach,
specialising in fresh fish. The
lower area is the best place for
those with kids, as they can play
in the sand while you eat. There
are also two floors inside and a
roof terrace. Sardines and salad
make an inexpensive lunch, but
otherwise you're looking at €20
per person and up.

Restaurante Três Coroas

Rua do Correiro Velho 8, Albufeira
☏ 289 512 640. Daily noon–3pm &
6.30–11pm. Tranquil place with a
leafy terrace with sea views and
a small aviary in one corner. The
short menu features decently
priced fish and meat dishes,
along with the house speciality
of sole cooked with bananas.
There's live music some nights,

which rather spoils the otherwise peaceful setting.

Bars and clubs

7½

Rua São Gonçalo de Lagos 5, Albufeira
☏ 289 585 431. Daily April–Sept Tues–
Sun 8pm–4am. Central Albufeira
bar and disco on a street full of
late-opening bars. Karaoke sessions and guest DJs sometimes
feature.

Bizarro Bar

Esplanada Dr. Frutuosa Silva 30, Albufeira ☏ 289 512 824. Mon–Sat 9am–1am.
This is a laid-back bar in a traditional, blue-faced building high
above the eastern end of the
beach, with superb views over
the sands from its front terrace.

Jo Jo's

Rua São Gonçalo de Lagos 1, Albufeira
☏ 289 588 762. Mon–Sat 10am–4pm
& 6.30pm–2am, Sun noon–4pm &
6.30pm–2am. Friendly family-
run pub with British soccer
and other sports on satellite
TV. It also serves pub-style
food, which always includes a
vegetarian option. The owner
proudly remembers the day Paul
Gascoigne and his mates got
hopelessly drunk here.

Kiss

Rua Vasco da Gama, Areias de São
João, Albufeira ☏ 282 515 639. May–
Sept daily midnight–6am; Oct–April
Sat & Sun midnight–6am. Out of
town, at the southern end of
Montechoro near the Forte
de São João, this is regarded as
the best club around town, and
often hosts foreign guest DJs,
but it tends to be overcrowded
and very glitzy; watch for posters
advertising events. You'll need to
rely on a taxi to get back to central Albufeira (around €6).

Café Latino

Rua Latino Coelho 59, Albufeira ☎289 585 132. Tues–Sun 10am–2am. With spinning ceiling fans, a snooker table and a back terrace with fantastic views, this is a superb spot to start off an evening. Along with the usual drinks there are exotic juice cocktails and snacks ranging from croissants to sandwiches and pizzas.

Portas da Vila

Rua da Bateria, Albufeira. Daily 1pm–1am. Built on the site of the former town gates, this high-ceilinged, traditionally decked-out bar lies just above the old fish market, with a few outdoor tables on the pedestrianized steps. The menu features a long list of cocktails and sangria.

Sir Harry's

Largo Eng. Duarte Pacheco 36–37, Albufeira ☎289 514 090. Daily 9am–3am. A mock pub in an attractive blue-and-white building on the main square, offering English breakfasts, light meals, live TV sports and a long list of cocktails.

Armação de Pêra and around

Armação de Pêra is one of the Algarve's most popular summer retreats for Portuguese holidaymakers, a bustling high-rise resort at the western end of a fantastic sweep of sand. The 10km or so of coast between Armação de Pêra and Centianes is flat and scrubby, fronting a series of delightful cove beaches that have somehow escaped any large-scale development. The relative inaccessibility of these beaches thins out the crowds, and they are conveniently linked by a fine clifftop coastal path. There are inland attractions, too, in the form of the pottery centre at Porches and The Big One water park.

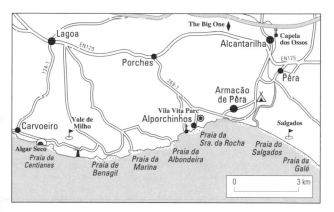

Armação de Pêra

Armação de Pêra is a major resort facing one of the longest beaches in the Algarve. The kernel of old buildings and the narrow, cobbled backstreets around the Praia dos Pescadores (Fishermen's Beach) are highly attractive, reminders of the time when fishermen from the village of Pêra, a couple of kilometres inland, used the once undeveloped beach to launch their *armação* – a combined fishing

---

Visiting Armação de Pêra

Armação de Pêra's bus terminal (☎282 315 781) is at the eastern end of the town and there are regular services from Albufeira, Portimão and Silves. The helpful turismo is on the seafront Avenida Marginal, ten minutes from the bus station (Mon–Fri 10am–1.30pm & 2.30–6pm; ☎282 312 145).

▲PROMENADE GARDENS, ARMAÇÃO DE PÊRA

boat netting system. The rest of Armação de Pêra is a characterless grid of ugly high-rises, with plenty more under construction. But facing the terraced gardens with its children's play area and cafés, it is easy to ignore the modern excesses. The remains of the town's fortified walls are at the eastern end of the seafront road, where a terrace in front of a little white chapel provides sweeping views. In summer, boat trips leave from Praia dos Pescadores to explore the area's fine caves and unusual rock formations to the west around Praia da Senhora da Rocha.

Alcantarilha

Alcantarilha is a surprisingly unspoilt town, considering its position on the EN125. Its main sight is its eighteenth-century Igreja Matriz, which contains a Capela dos Ossos, a chapel lined with the bones of around 1500 humans, similar to that in Faro (see p.54). These chapels were partly a practical solution to lack of cemetery space. Unfortunately the chapel opens only occasionally, though at such times entry is free.

The Big One

ⓦ www.bigone-waterpark.com; May–Sept daily 10am–5.30pm; €16, children €13. Beyond Alcantarilha just off the EN125, the Big

One is a giant water park set among lawns and palms, with an array of pools and slides with apt names such as "Labyrinth", "Crazy leap" and "Kamikaze". Best of all is the "Banzai Boggan", a terrifying 23-metre, near-vertical slide into water.

Porches

The pleasant if unexceptional village of Porches is famous for its hand-painted pottery (majolica). The chunky, hand-painted majolica-ware employs glazing techniques used since Moorish times. Workshops – usually open daily – line the main EN125, although not all the goods on sale are produced in Porches; you can find everything from Barcelos pots from northern Portugal to wood-burning ovens and *azulejos*-inlaid table tops, which can be shipped abroad if required. A good place to browse is Casa Algarve (ⓣ282 352 682, daily 9.30am–6.30pm), just west of Porches, set in a late nineteenth-century former restaurant with an *azulejo*-lined back patio.

Praia da Albondeira and Praia da Marinha

Occasional buses from Lagoa; by car, turn south off the EN125, between Porches and Lagoa, opposite the International School. The attractive beach of Praia da Albondeira

marks the start of a superb ninety-minute coastal foot-path which stretches west for 4km all the way to the pretty village of Benagil (see below). Even more alluring is Praia da Marinha, nestling below a craggy red sandstone cliff, with the only trace of development being a tasteful villa complex a little up the hill. To reach the beach from the neatly tended car park, descend the cobbled track that leads off to the left from the clifftop picnic tables. The beach has a simple seasonal café-restaurant.

Benagil

Benagil is a tiny fishing village with a cluster of build-ings above a narrow gully. The road loops down over a dried-up river valley, at the bottom of which, under high cliffs, is a fine beach dotted with fishing boats. Ask around and the fishermen are usually happy to take you out to see the nearby caves, some of the most spectacular in the Algarve, for around €10.

▲PHAIA DA MARINHA

Praia de Centianes

Reached by some lengthy steps, Praia de Centianes, to the west of Benagil, is a fine beach set below sculpted cliffs, with its own café-restaurant right on the sands. However, as it's backed by a fair amount of development,

▼BENAGIL

the sands can get very crowded in high season.

Accommodation

Hotel Garbe

Avda Beira Mar 1, Armação de Pêra ☎282 315 187, ⊛hotelgarbe.com. A few minutes' walk west of the tourist office, this modern block has a prime site facing the beach. Rooms are varied, although most have balconies. The hotel also has a pool, TV and games room, in-house Indian restaurant and a baby-sitting service. €126, or €216 for sea views.

Vila Linda Mar

Benagil ☎282 352 812, ⊛algarve-paradise.com. In a rural setting 1km east of Benagil, *Vila Linda Mar* is a tasteful, traditionally dec-orated guesthouse with its own lawns and a small pool. There are just a handful of rooms, all with bathrooms, TVs and fridges; the best ones with balconies offer distant sea views. Also has a fine restaurant (see opposite). €85, or €95 for sea views.

Vila Vita Parc

Alporchinhos ☎282 310 100, ⊛www.vilavitaparc.com.Two kilometres west of Armação de Pêra and spreading above its own beaches, this is a five-star holiday resort in palm-lined grounds dotted with pools, fountains and sports facilities: there's even a helipad, which says something about its guests.The hotel and villas are built in traditional Portuguese style – all terracotta roof tiles and *azulejos* – and facilities include a variety of restaurants (including one specially for families with kids), a health club, state-of-the-art gym and spa. €460.

Campsite

Parque de Campismo de Armação de Pêra

Armação de Pêra ☎282 312 904 ⊛www.roteiro-campista.pt. Around 1km north of town, this well-equipped campsite has its own pool, supermarket, restaurant and gardens.

Cafés

Esplanade Bar Mini Golf

Avda Marginal , Armação de Pêra ☎282 312 414. Mon, Tues & Thurs–Sun 10am–10pm. Near the tourist office, with outside tables on a terrace overlooking the beach. The perfect place to watch the sun go down over a Superbock or two, or if this is too sedate, there's an outdoor games area complete with children's rides, table football and minigolf.

Restaurants

O Algar

Benagil ☎282 358 951. Tues–Sun noon–3pm & 6.30–10pm.On the approach road to Benagil from the east, this restaurant has a lovely leafy terrace and serves moderately priced dishes such as *cataplana* and *arroz de tamboril* (monkfish rice).

Estrela do Mar

Praia dos Pescadores, Armação de Pêra ☎282 313 775. Tues–Sun 11am–3pm & 6pm–midnight. Right on the fishermen's beach nestled among the boats, this simple beach shack offers bargain Portuguese staples (under €10 for a full meal); the *sardinhas assada* (grilled sardines) are superb.

Rocha da Palha

Largo da Fortaleza, Armação de Pêra
☎965 016 615. Daily 11am–3pm & 7–
11pm. Inexpensive grilled fish and
meat – including some fine rice
dishes – can be enjoyed here on
a little terrace facing the beach.

O Serol

Rua Portas do Mar 2, Armação de Pêra
☎282 312 146. Mon, Tues & Thurs–
Sun noon–3.30pm & 6–10.30pm.
Just east of the church near the
fishermen's beach, with a cosy
interior and an outdoor terrace,
this is one of the town's best and
not too pricey fish restaurants
(€15–20 for a full meal), full of
trussed lobsters and crabs. It also
lets out inexpensive rooms.

Vila Linda Mar

Benagil ☎282 352 812. Mon &
Wed–Sun 7–10.30pm. Rural
restaurant 1km east of Benagil,
serving superb, mid-priced
Algarvian dishes such as *presunto
de Monchique* (smoked ham from
Monchique) and *gambas com
espinafres* (prawns with spinach).
It doubles as a hotel (see
opposite).

Carvoeiro and around

The former fishing village of Carvoeiro has developed into a firm favourite for package holidays, and its centre of fishermen's houses spilling down a hillside to the beach is backed by substantial development. Out of season the town has more appeal, and it is within easy range of the attractions of Estômbar and the Slide and Splash water park. Some of the region's finest cove beaches can be found on the less-developed coastline between Carvoeiro and Ferragudo, another attractive former fishing village on the Rio Arade estuary. However, bear in mind that there are virtually no public transport connections to these beaches, so you'll need a car to reach them.

Carvoeiro

Cut into the red cliffs and clustered round a sandy cove, Carvoeiro was once one of the Algarve's prettiest fishing villages. Today it has grown into a somewhat rambling resort and its beach struggles to cope with the summer crowds, but with a plethora of cafés and restaurants and a busy nightlife it's anything but dull.

▼CARVOEIRO

Visiting Carvoeiro

Regular buses call at Carvoeiro from Portimão and Armação de Pêra, though some involve a change at Lagoa. The turismo (mid-Sept to May Mon–Fri 9.30am–1pm & 2–5.30pm; June to mid-Sept daily 9.30am–7pm; ☏282 357 728), just behind the beach, can give details of private rooms. To get around, a toy train passes round town and out to Algar Seco and Praia de Centianes (see p.121) every twenty minutes (€3 round trip).

Algar Seco

One kilometre east from Carvoeiro along the coast road are the impressive rock formations of Algar Seco, where steps down the cliffs pass sculpted rocks, pillars and blowholes above slapping waves. There's a small café-bar, *Boneca* (March–Sept daily 10am–dusk), which is named after the neighbouring A Boneca, a rock window reached through a short tunnel, offering neatly framed sea views. Boat trips from Portimão (see p.137), often stop off here.

Estômbar

Take any stopping train on the Algarve line. Also served by regular bus from Portimão. A few kilometres north-west of Carvoeiro is the little town of Estômbar. Once an important Moorish settlement thriving on salt production, it was also the birthplace of the eleventh-century Moorish poet Ibn Ammâr. While the town today is unremarkable, straggling down a steep hill in a confusion of narrow lanes, it's free from tourist trappings. The most interesting sight is the church, the Igreja de Sant'Iago, which looks like a diminutive version of the superb abbey church at Alcobaça north of Lisbon. The interior has superb eight-eenth-century *azulejos* and two Manueline sculpted columns carved with exotic plants and vines.

Slide and Splash

Around 3km outside Estômbar, sign-posted off the EN125 at Vale de Deus. Served by 1–2 daily buses from most nearby resorts, including Carvoeiro, Albufeira and Armação de Pêra. ☏282 341 685, ⊛www.slidesplash.com. Daily April–Oct 10am–5pm. €15.50, children €12.50. For a change from the beach, the varied water chutes, flumes, slides, pools and aquatic fun at the Slide & Splash theme park make a great half day or so, especially for older kids.

▼ALGAR SECO

▲FERRAGUDO

Praia da Caneiros

The idyllic cove beach of Praia da Caneiros sits below cliffs with soft sand and a smart café-restaurant. Just off the beach, a rock stack known as Leixão das Gaivotas juts into view, usually flecked with rows of basking cormorants.

Praia Pintadinho

Praia Pintadinho is a lovely cliff-backed cove beach, with its own café-restaurant. The sandy cove has rock caves at either end to shelter from the sun. Scramble up the rocks to the east of the bay and there are some fine clifftop walks along the coast; within five minutes you reach a small lighthouse, with views to Ponta da Piedade to the west and, on clear days, as far as the Sagres peninsula.

Praia Grande

Praia Grande lies within Portimão's harbour walls, on the opposite side of the estuary to the town. Meaning "big beach", this fine stretch of broad sands has its western end dotted with restaurants, though the eastern end is quieter.

Ferragudo

Regular buses from Portimão. Ferragudo, facing Portimão across the estuary, is one of the least spoilt former fishing villages on this stretch of the Algarve. Although many of the old fishermen's cottages have been snapped up by wealthy Lisboans and ex-pats, few concessions have been made to international tourism and the village retains its traditional character. The town spreads round a strip of palm-fringed gardens running alongside a narrow riverlet up to the cobbled main square, Praça Rainha Dona Leonor, dotted with cafés. Just west of here, the riverlet ends at the Rio Arade estuary, where a promenade skirts a small fishing harbour and a row of fish restaurants. South of here, a warren of atmospheric cobbled backstreets wend their way up the side of a hill to the town's church, parts of which date back to the fourteenth century; there are great views over the estuary to Portimão from the church terrace. Running along the foot of the hill below the church – accessible at low tide from the fishing harbour or by taking the road that skirts the old town – lies the town beach – Angrinha – a thin stretch of sand which gets progressively more appealing as it approaches the **Castelo de São João do Arade**. The sixteenth-century fort, one of a pair to defend the Rio Arade (the other is opposite in Praia da Rocha, see p.137), sits impressively right on the sands. Remodelled in the early twentieth century by the resident poet Coelho Carvalho, it is currently in private hands.

Accommodation

Algar Seco Parque

Rua das Flores, Algar Seco ☎282 350 440, ⊛www.algarseco.pt. A series of tasteful studios, apartments and villas spill down terraced gardens above the Algar Seco rocks. There's a pool, bar and restaurant, and each room is well equipped and tastefully furnished in traditional Portuguese stye. Studios from €122.

Hotel Carvoeiro Sol

Carvoeiro ☎282 357 301, ⓔcarvoeirosol@mail.telepac.pt. Comfortable if unimaginative four-star concrete block right by the beach. Rooms come with small balconies, though you pay around €25 extra for sea views. There's also a pool, courtyard bar and a baby-sitting service. €144.

Casabela Hotel

Praia Grande ☎282 490 650, ⊛www .hotel-casabela.com. Well worth a splurge, the *Casabela Hotel* is set in a low modern building with fantastic grounds above Praia Grande and a short walk from Praia Pintadinho. Most rooms have wonderful views, and

there's a heated pool, bar, tennis courts and disabled access. €165.

O Castelo

Rua da Casino 59–61, Carvoeiro ☎ & ☎282 357 416, ⓔcasteloguesthouse@clix.pt. Overlooking the beach, five minutes' walk uphill from the tourist office, this is the budget option in town, but book ahead as there are just three rooms. Each is clean and modern with superb views; two have their own balconies. The price does not include breakfast. €50.

Quinta da Horta

Ferragudo ☎282 461 395, ⓔart-ferragudo@clix.pt. Around 1km east of town, this charming place is run by a British artist who also runs art courses – and the occasional naturist gathering. A series of tasteful spartan rooms and a self-catering apartment (sleeps four) are set round a tropical garden with a small pond. There's a little plunge pool, a sauna, TV room and tennis court, and three horses for treks or for picnics in a gypsy cart. A superb organic breakfast is included in the price; evening meals on request. €65, apartment €115.

Vila Castelo

Angrinha, Apartado 33, Ferragudo ☎282 461 993, UK bookings on ☎01604 584888 ⊛www.vilacastelo .com. Modern, British-run upmarket apartment complex on the hillside opposite the castle, a five-minute walk from the old town church. Apartments are well equipped with smart kitchens and satellite TV; the best ones have balconies or terraces with superb views over the castle. There's also a communal pool. One-week minimum let in high season. €90.

Campsite

Parque Campismo de Ferragudo

☎282 461 121, ✆www.roteiro-campista.pt. This privately run campsite, 3km east of Ferragudo between Praia Pintadinho and Praia da Caneiros, is only open to those with an International Camping Carnet. It's very well equipped with a pool, kids' play area, large supermarket and a restaurant. There's usually plenty of space for tents beneath the trees.

Cafés

Gelataria A Pérola

Praça Rainha D. Leonor 12–13, Ferragudo ☎282 461 411. Daily 8am–9pm, June–Sept until midnight. Filled with families at weekends, this is the best spot for ice cream and pastries; sunny seats spill out onto the square.

Restaurants

O Barco

Largo da Praia, Carvoeiro ☎282 357 975. Mon, Tues & Thurs–Sun 10am–midnight. Unexceptional, reasonably priced food – from snacks to Portuguese dishes and pasta – with an excellent position facing the sands.

O Barril

Trav do Caldeirão 1–5, Ferragudo ☎282 461 215. Mon, Tues & Thurs–Sun noon–2pm & 7pm–2am. Tucked under the arches in an alley just off the main square, this bar-restaurant serves unexceptional and pricey seafood and fish (mains around €15), but it does offer live Fado sessions most nights from 8pm.

O Castelo

Rua da Casino 63, Carvoeiro ☎282 357 218. Tues–Sun 6.30–10.30pm. Below the guesthouse of the same name, this is a slightly pricey place for standard Portuguese food, but it does boast a great terrace overlooking the beach.

Escondidinho

Praia Grande ☎282 461 037. Daily: Oct–May 11am–5pm; June–Sept daily 10am–midnight. The "little hidden one" is to the right of the steps down to the beach. Little more than a shack and an outdoor terrace with views over the beach and Ferragudo's castle, it offers a change with an international medley of inexpensive dishes such as mushrooms in batter, lasagne and moussaka.

Pintadinho

Praia Pintadinho ☎282 461 659. Late March–Oct daily 10am–dusk (until midnight in July and Aug). This simple beachside café-restaurant sits right on the sands; snacks and drinks are well priced but seafood and fish, though tasty, are expensive. The wonderful sea views, however, make it all worthwhile.

Rei das Praias

Praia da Caneiros ☎282 461 006. March–Oct daily 10am–10pm. On stilts above the beach, this is rated as one of the Algarve's best beachside restaurants, with meals served either on the terrace or in the swish interior. There is a fine wine list and expensive but superb dishes include prawns cooked in piri-piri sauce and fish baked in salt. Upwards of €20 for a full meal.

Sueste

Rua da Ribeira 91, Ferragudo ☎282 461 592. Tues–Sun 12.30–3pm & 7–

▲ESTÔMBAR BACKSTREETS

11pm. The most arty and buzzy of a row of fish restaurants facing the harbour. Superior if pricey fish dishes are served on an outdoor terrace or a cosy interior.

O Velho Novo

Rua Manuel Teixeira Gomes 2, Ferragudo. Daily 6pm–1am. Five minutes' walk from the main square – cross the rivulet along the road signed to Belavista and it's on the left – this good-value option offers fish and meats grilled on an outside barbecue. You can eat at tables inside or sit out on wooden benches; full meals cost under €15.

Bars

La Be

Rua Vasco da Gama 33, Ferragudo. Mon, Tues, Thurs, Fri & Sun 0pm 4am, Sat 5pm–4am. One of Ferragudo's livelier bars, with pub-like decor; down by the harbour.

Clubs

Bote Disco Club

Largo do Carvoeiro, Carvoeiro ☎282 357 285. June–Sept Tues–Sun 11pm–6am; Oct–May Sat only. Lively and fun nightclub on a prime coastal spot, with a beach-facing terrace for a breather between the contemporary sounds.

Silves and around

Surrounded by orange groves and dominated by a Moorish castle, Silves is the Algarve's most enticing inland town. Under the Moors, Silves, then called Xelb, was capital of the al-Gharb and had a population three times the current one, though many of its finer buildings were destroyed in the earthquake of 1755. Today it is a pleasant market town, with a series of bustling cobbled streets leading up from the riverfront to the small leafy central square, Praça do Município. Alongside, the Torreão das Portas da Cidade – the remains of the Moorish town gate – mark the extent of the oldest parts of town, which is dominated by the cathedral and the imposing fortress. Silves sits in the heart of some picturesque countryside, best enjoyed at the reservoir, Barragem do Arade.

▼HEADING UP TO THE SÉ, SILVES

The riverfront

Down on the riverfront, near the narrow thirteenth-century bridge, Silves' market (Mon–Sat 8am–1pm) has some fine outdoor grill-cafés (see p.134) where you can sit and watch life go by. The river valley opposite here is still cultivated, the fields dotted with superbly fragrant orange trees.

The fortress

Daily: July–Aug 9am–8pm; Sept–June 9am–6pm; last entry 30min before closing time. €1.25, under-12s free. The Moorish fortress remains the focal point of Silves with an impressively complete set of sandstone walls and towers. It is currently undergoing extensive renovation, which will eventually re-create a Moorish-style garden, a traditional well and the governor's palace; work is

Visiting Silves

The train station lies 2km south of town; there are occasional connecting buses or it's an easy walk. Arriving by bus, you'll be dropped on the main road at the foot of the town near the riverfront, next to the market. During the summer, regular boat trips pass up the Rio Arade to Silves from Portimão; see p.137.

The regional turismo is at Rua 25 de Abril 26–28 (Mon–Sat 10am–1.30pm & 2.30–6pm, until 7pm in July–Sept; ☎282 442 255); the town hall also runs a tourism information kiosk on Largo de Município (Mon–Fri 9.30am–1pm & 2–5.30pm; ☎282 442 325) and can give out details of local events.

scheduled to finish in 2006. Renovation also restricts access to the wonderful vaulted thirteenth-century water cistern, the Cisterna Grande, that once served the town. Some 10m in height and supported by six columns, the cistern is said to be haunted by a Moorish maiden who can be seen sailing across the underground waters during a full moon. However, you can still clamber onto the castle walls for impressive views over the town and surrounding hills.

The Sé

Mon–Sat 8.30am–6.30pm, Sun limited hours between Mass. Free. Silves' cathedral, or Sé, sits below the fortress, an impressive thir-teenth-century edifice built on the site of the Grand Mosque. Between 1242 and 1577, this was the Algarve's most important church, but the bishopric was moved to Faro when Silves lost its role as a major port. Flanked by broad Gothic towers, it has a suitably defiant, military appearance, though the Great Earthquake and poor restoration since have left the interior less impressive than the exterior. The tombs lining the cathedral walls are of bishops and of Crusaders who died taking Silves back from the Moors.

Opposite the Sé is the newer Igreja da Misericórdia (Mon–Fri 9.30am–1pm & 2–5.30pm; free), a sixteenth-century church with

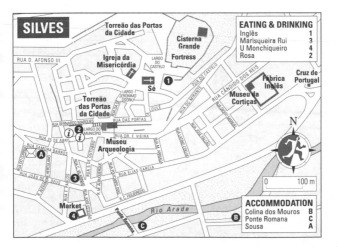

Moorish Silves

Under the Moors, Silves was a thriving port and a place of grandeur, described in contemporary accounts as "of shining brightness" within its three dark circuits of guarding walls. It was also famed for its artistic community, and in the tenth century it was considered culturally more important than Granada, the leading Moorish city in Spain. Its greatness largely ended in 1189, with the arrival of Sancho I at the head of a mixed army of Crusaders, and Silves permanently fell to Christian forces in 1249. The gradual silting up of the Rio Arade over the next few centuries ended Silves' role as one of the great cultural centres of Iberia.

a fine Manueline doorway and hung with seven impressive religious images, painted on wood.

Museu Arqueologia

Rua da Porta de Loulé ☎282 444 832. Mon–Sat 9am–6pm. €1.50. Despite a lack of English-language labelling, the archaeological museum is an engaging collection, containing various remains from Silves and the surrounding area. There are Stone Age pillars, Roman pots and coins

▼THE SÉ, SILVES

and beautiful Moorish and later Portuguese ceramics. Upstairs, the temporary exhibition hall offers a great vantage point for looking down into the 10m-deep Moorish well, left in situ in the basement. You can also go out onto parts of the old town walls, which offer fine views over the town.

Fábrica de Inglês

Rua Gregório Mascarenhas ☎282 440 480, ⊕www.fabrica-do-ingles.com. Tues–Sun 12.30–3pm & 7–10.30pm. Free except during special events, when hours and charges vary. The Fabrica Inglês (English Factory) is an exhibition centre-cum-theme park set in a former cork factory, opened in 1894 by a three-man team from Catalonia, Silves and England (hence the name). A series of cafés and bars are clustered round a delightful central courtyard filled with outdoor tables below scented orange trees. It is most animated when it hosts the annual summer Silves **Beer Festival**, usually in July, and on Friday nights when there are special events, including sound and light shows. It also incorporates the **Museu da Cortiça** (☎282 440 440; Mon–Sun 9.30am–12.45pm & 2–6.15pm; €2), a small cork museum. There are a few evocative black-and-white photos of local cork cutters, but unless you have a keen interest

▲BARRAGEM DO ARADE

in the cork industry, it's unlikely to set your pulse racing.

Barragem do Arade

Set in tranquil woodland, the Barragem do Arade is a popular spot with campervanners and is a fine place to visit for a swim, walk or some more exerting water sports, though you'll need your own transport to get here. There are various *barragems*, or reservoirs, dotted round the Algarve, and this is one of the area's main sources of water set amongst rolling, tree-lined hills. It's a bucolic spot popular with migrating birds, though when the water level falls in summer the barren sides of the exposed mountains spoil the picturesque effect.

Just as the dam itself comes into view, take the left-hand fork in the road to *Café Coutada* (see p.134) which can organize boat trips to a scraggy, tree-lined offshore islet known – rather generously – as Paradise Island. The fee (€7.50, children €6.50) covers the return boat trip together with use of canoes, sun loungers, and swimming in cordoned-off areas of the reservoir (as the reservoir is a water supply, swimming elsewhere is discouraged). You can also hire jet skis.

Accommodation

Hotel Colina dos Mouros

Silves ⊕ 282 440 420, ⊕ 282 440 426. The most comfortable accommodation in town, in a modern hotel over the bridge from the fortress. The pleasant rooms have TVs and spotless bathrooms, and there's an outdoor pool in the small, tranquil grounds. €80.

Residencial Ponte Romana

Ponte Romana, Silves ⊕ 282 443 275. Reached by the old pedestrian bridge over the river, this simple guest house has rather poky rooms with their own bathrooms; the best ones face the river. The price does not include breakfast. €30.

Quinta do Rio

Sítio São Estevão, Apartado 217 ⊕ & ⊕ 282 445 528. Around 5km out of Silves, off the road to São Bartolomeu de Messines, this country inn has six delightful, rustic-style rooms with passionflower-shaded terraces facing open country. Breakfast consists of fresh fruit grown on the farm, and the Italian owners can supply evening meals on request. €52.

Residencial Sousa

Rua Samora Barros 17, Silves
☎282 442 502. Plain, faded rooms
with shared bathrooms in an
attractive town house a couple
of blocks up from the riverfront.
€30.

Cafés

Café Coutada

Barragem do Arade. Daily 10am–10pm.
Facing the reservoir, this well-
positioned café surrounded by
aviaries offers decent if slightly
pricey drinks and meals on an
outdoor terrace.

Pastelaria Rosa

Largo do Município, Silves ☎282
442 255. Daily 8am–10pm. Superb
old *pastelaria* with cool interior
stone walls covered in *azulejos*
and a counter groaning with
cakes and goodies. Outdoor
tables spill onto the pretty main
square next to the fountain.

Café Inglês

Escadas do Castelo, Silves ☎282
442 585. Mon noon–3pm, Tues–Fri
noon–11pm, Sat 6.30pm–10pm.
Beautifully done-up 1900s town
house with a back terrace and
tables spilling onto the cobbles
outside. Choose from moderately priced drinks and snacks
to full meals. On Friday and
Saturday nights there's often live
Latin American or jazz music,
while from June to September
the roof terrace opens for pizzas.
It also hosts occasional art exhibitions.

Restaurants

Restaurante Marisqueira Rui

Rua Comendador Vilarinho, Silves
☎282 442 682. Mon & Wed–Sun
noon–3pm & 7–10pm. Despite its
inland position, this is one of the
Algarve's best seafood restaurants, with prices to match. It's
very popular, so arrive early to
guarantee a table as it is perenni-
ally popular.

U Monchiqueiro

Mercado, Silves. Mon, Tues & Thurs–
Sun noon–3pm & 7–11pm. The
best of a handful of inexpensive grill-cafés by the market.
Tuck into inexpensive piri-piri
chicken, fries, salad and wine
outside, or under the awnings
for live soccer on TV. Around
€10 for a full meal.

▼CAFÉ INGLÊS, SILVES

Portimão, Praia da Rocha and around

Large and functional, Portimão is not particularly hand-some, but it remains the best place to catch a boat trip up the coast, and its largely pedestrianized central streets make it one of the area's better places for shop-pers. Virtually a suburb of Portimão, Praia da Rocha was one of the first Algarve tourist developments thanks to its enormous, broad sandy beach, framed by jagged rock formations and a clifftop fort, and it remains one of the region's most visited resorts. There are fine beaches to be enjoyed west of Portimão at Praia do Vau and Praia de Três Irmãos, which merges with the best stretch of sand at Praia de Alvor. The latter peters out at the estu-ary of the Rio de Alvor, where the town of Alvor, an erstwhile fishing vil-lage with a characterful riverfront harbour, lies close to the Quinta da Rocha seabird refuge.

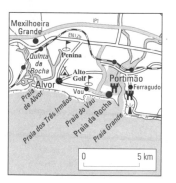

Portimão centre

Known as Portus Magnus in Roman times, Portimão became a major departure point for the great Portuguese explorers: Bartolomeu Dias set off from here in 1487 to become the first European to round the southern tip of Africa. But the modern town of Portimão is dominated by pedestrianized shopping streets and graceless concrete high-rises – most of the older buildings were destroyed in the 1755 earthquake. The most historic building is the Igreja da Nossa Senhora da Conceição, rebuilt after the earthquake but retaining a Manueline door

▼PORTIMÃO SHOPPING STREETS

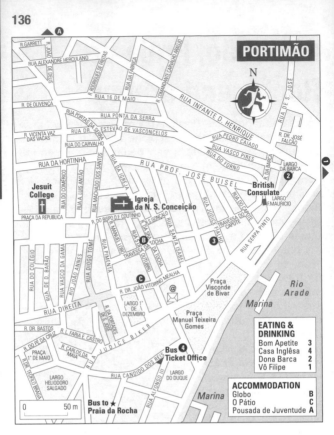

from the original fourteenth-century structure; the interior is more impressive, with three aisles and a vaulted ceiling. The walls are covered in seventeenth-century decorative *azulejos*.

The encircling streets are pleasant enough, filled with shops catering to the day-trippers – selling lace, shoes, jewellery, ceramics and wicker goods; the main shopping streets are around the pedestrianized Rua Diogo Tomé and Rua da Portades de São José. Just off the latter lies Largo 1 de Dezembro, an atmospheric square with benches

Visiting Portimão

The train station is inconveniently located at the northern tip of town on Largo Ferra Prado. From here a bus runs every 45 minutes (Mon–Fri) into the centre; a taxi costs about €4, or it's a fifteen-minute walk. Buses (including those to and from Praia da Rocha) pull up much more centrally, in the streets around the Largo do Duque, close to the river. The turismo is on Cais do Comércio e Turismo, just back from the riverfront on the road to Praia da Rocha (☎282 416 556; Mon–Sat 10am–5.30pm).

▲GRILLED SARDINES THIS WAY, PORTIMÃO

inlaid with *azulejos* depicting Portuguese historical scenes, including Pedro Álvares Cabral's landing in Brazil in 1500.

Portimão riverfront

The most attractive part of town is the riverfront gardens, a series of squares – Largo do Duque, Praça Manuel Teixeira Gomes, and Praça Visconde de Bivar – with bustling cafés beneath shady trees right by the river. Along here, you'll be approached by people offering boat trips along the coast to see weird and wonderful grottoes, including trips to Carvoeiro, Lagos and even up the Rio Arade to Silves.

Heading under the road bridge, you'll find a series of open-air restaurants serving inexpensive grilled sardine lunches.

The streets just back from the bridge – off Largo da Barca – are Portimão's oldest: narrow, cobbled and with more than a hint of their fishing-quarter past. Largo da Barca itself is a lovely little hidden square, lined with tables from various upmarket fish restaurants (see pp.142–43).

Praia da Rocha

Praia da Rocha ("beach of rock") is something of a misnomer as, despite the low cliffs and jagged rocks around it, the beach here is one of the deepest stretches of sand in the Algarve. Sadly, it is backed by rather characterless high-rise hotels, discos and a casino, though here and there among the hotel blocks fin-de-siècle villas testify to the resort's more upmarket

▼PRAIA DA ROCHA

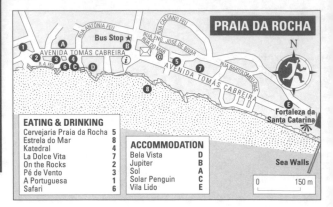

PRAIA DA ROCHA

N

Bus Stop ★

EATING & DRINKING

Cervejaria Praia da Rocha	5
Estrela do Mar	8
Katedral	4
La Dolce Vita	7
On the Rocks	2
Pé de Vento	3
A Portuguesa	1
Safari	6

ACCOMMODATION

Bela Vista	D
Jupiter	B
Sol	A
Solar Penguin	C
Vila Lido	E

Fortaleza da
Santa Catarina

Sea Walls

0   150 m

past. Most of the modern development is channelled into a strip just two blocks wide north of the main street, Avenida Tomás Cabreira; from the *avenida* steep steps lead down to the sands.

The west end of the beach is marked by a *miradouro* with further views up the coast, though this end of Avenida Tomás Cabreira is tackier and more commercialized than the eastern end.

Fortaleza da Santa Caterina

The low walls of the Fortaleza da Santa Caterina cap the eastern end of the Avenida Tomás Cabreira. Built in 1691 to protect the mouth of the River Arade, the fort offers splendid views at sunset – beach and ocean on one side, Ferragudo, the marina and river

on the other; there's also a small garden below the fort with great views back over the beach. Down the steep steps to the beach below the castle, you can walk out along the harbour walls for more great views back to the fort.

Vau, Praia de Três Irmãos and Praia de Alvor

Regular daily buses run from Portimão to Alvor along the coastal stretch, calling at all the beaches en route. Vau is an undistinguished resort facing a lovely, typically Algarvian beach backed by rock pillars and cliffs. The town's apartments make up a fairly characterless settlement, but there are plenty of clifftop restaurants if you fancy stopping for a meal.

Separated by a rocky headland – which you can walk round

Visiting Praia da Rocha

Bus connections from Portimão depart every fifteen to thirty minutes, leaving from the stop just south of Largo do Duque (daily 7.30am–11.30pm; €1.50 single). If you plan to do much to-ing and fro-ing between Rocha and Portimão, buy a block of ten tickets from a kiosk in Portimão, and you'll save around fifty percent on the fare.

The turismo (May to mid-Sept 9.30am–7pm; mid-Sept to April Mon & Fri–Sun 10am–1.30pm & 2.30–6pm, Tues–Thurs 9.30am–6pm; ☏282 419 132) is right by the beach.

Visiting Alvor

Regular buses (roughly hourly) run to Alvor from Portimão. The turismo is in the centre of town at Rua Dr. Alfonso Costa 51 (daily: June–Sept 9.30am–7pm; Oct–May 10am–1.30pm & 2.30–6pm; ☏282 457 540).

in twenty minutes or so – lies another fine stretch of sands, Praia de Três Irmãos, which becomes Praia de Alvor. Both beaches are backed by villas and hotels, especially at the eastern end, but there's usually enough space to lay your towel with a little privacy, even in high season.

Alvor

Alvor was a sleepy fishing village until the 1960s but has grown into quite a popular resort, and modern, low-rise buildings now outnumber its Moorish core. Although much of the town was razed in the 1755 earthquake, it still boasts a sixteenth-century **Igreja Matriz** with superb Manueline doors, arches and pillars carved into fishing ropes and exotic plants. The old core around the church and the central Praça da

República is the most enjoyable and atmospheric part of town, and the harbour itself is a delight, lined with colourful fishing boats and aromatic fish restaurants.

You can still make out the vestiges of Alvor's thirteenth-century castle, now a leafy ruin with a children's playground. Opposite the castle lies the small covered fruit and vegetable market, which is usually animated from 7am (Mon–Sat).

Alvor's liveliest street is Rua Dr. Frederico Romas Mendes, lined with bars and restaurants and culminating in a pedestrianized square, Largo da Ribeiro, right on the riverside. The square is marked by a quirky modern statue of a fish, appropriately marking the old fish market (now deserted) and faced by half a dozen excellent fish restaurants. The views here

▼ALVOR WATERFRONT

▲QUINTA DA ROCHA

and almond groves, protects copses, salt marshes, sandy spits and estuarine mud flats, all offering a wide range of habitats for different plants and animals – including 22 species of wading bird. Flanked by the Penina Golf Club to the northeast and the Palmares Golf Club to the west (see pp.28–29), the area remains vulnerable as protected status has not been secured, despite attempts by environmentalists; for the time being, however, development is being kept at bay.

With a car, the best approach to the reserve is along the small turning off the EN125 opposite Mexilheira Grande, signed Benavides/Quinta da Rocha. Within the nature area there are plenty of narrow roads and tracks to wander around the estuary and see wading birds and clam fishermen.

are wonderful, overlooking the picturesque estuary of the Rio Alvor, swooped over by seagulls and lined with beached fishing boats. Head right as you face the river and a walkway leads up the estuary for an attractive *passeio*; head left and ten minutes' walk past cafés and the fishermen's huts you reach the extensive sands of Praia de Alvor.

Quinta da Rocha nature area

The Quinta da Rocha nature area lies on a peninsula between the mouths of the rivers Alvor and Odiáxere, northwest of Alvor's huge beach. It is an extensive area which, in the parts not given over to citrus

Accommodation

Hotel Bela Vista

Avda Tomás Cabreira, Praia da Rocha ☏282 450 480, ⊛www.hotelbelavista .net. The most stylish place to stay on the seafront, this pseudo-Moorish mansion was built in 1903; the interior is an exquisite mixture of carved woods, stained glass, and yellow, white and blue *azulejos*. Rooms are large and airy and there's a great downstairs beach-facing terrace. €115.

Hospedaria Buganvilia

Rua Padre Mendes Rossio de 5 Pedro, Lote 2, Alvor ☏282 459 412. Just down the hill from the turismo, this modern guesthouse offers spotless en-suite rooms, most with balconies. There's also a roof terrace and a decent downstairs restaurant. Minimum one week's stay in high season. €65.

Casa Três Palmeiras

Apt. 84, Praia do Vau ☎282 401 275, ☻www.casatrespalmeiras.com. Closed Dec–Jan. In an idyllic position on a clifftop above a little beach, this sleek villa is a superb example of 1960s design chic. Its glass-fronted rooms curve round a terrace with its own pool where breakfast is served in summer. Rooms and communal areas are spacious and tastefully furnished in traditional Portuguese style. Services include manicures, reflexology and massages on request, and discounts are available for local golf courses. €100.

Dom João II

Praia de Alvor ☎282 400 700, ☻www .pestana.com. Around 1km from Alvor, facing the beach, this high-rise four-star is very comfortable but soulless. There's a large pool, kids' club and restaurant, and guests have discounts at the nearby Tennis Country Club and the Pinta and Gramacha Golf Courses. In low season, prices are reduced by up to fifty percent. Disabled access. €188.

Hotel Globo

Rua 5 de Outubro, Apartado 151, Portimão ☎282 416 350, ☻282 483 142. Good-value modern highrise close to the Igreja Matriz. The decor is dull, but it has its own restaurant and top rooms overlook the harbour. €95.

Hotel Jupiter

Avda Tomás Cabreira, Praia da Rocha ☎282 415 041, ☻hoteljupiter@mail .telepac.pt. A modern hulk on the wrong (land) side of the avenida; comfortable rooms, with disabled access, but you pay €15 extra for sea views. There's also a bar, restaurant and small outdoor pool. €115.

Residencial O Pátio

Rua Dr. João Vitorino Mealha 3, Portimão ☎282 424 288, ☻282 424 281. Characterful guesthouse, with simple en-suite rooms done up in traditional Portuguese style, as is the characterful little downstairs bar-breakfast room. There's an outside patio, too. Price does not include breakfast. €45.

Residencial Sol

Avda Tomás Cabreira 10, Praia da Rocha ☎282 424 071, ☻282 419 944. Standard but good-value rooms in a modern block opposite the Katedral nightclub – so pick from noisy rooms with sea views or quieter ones without much to look at. €50.

Solar Penguin

Rua António Feu, Praia da Rocha ☎ & ☻282 424 308. Closed mid-Nov to mid-Jan. Right on the cliffs above the beach, this delightful if faintly shabby pensão has large, airy rooms overlooking the sea. €50.

Residencial Vila Lido

Avda Tomás Cabreira, Praia da Rocha ☎282 424 127, ☻282 424 246. This beautiful blue-shuttered building with original, traditional Portuguese decor sits in the less tacky east end of the avenida in its own small grounds facing the fort; front rooms (€10 extra) have superb views over the beach. €75.

Youth hostel

Lugar do Coca, Maravilhas, Portimão ☎ & ☻282 491 804. Well-equipped, large, modern hostel with its own small swimming pool, bar, canteen, and sports facilities that include snooker and tennis courts. There are plenty of dorm rooms (sleeping four; €10) and a handful of double rooms (€29).

Campsite

Parque de Campismo Dourado

Estrada Monte de Alvor, Alvor ☎282 459 178, ⊛www.roteiro-campista.pt. Around 1km north of Alvor, this is a pleasant leafy campsite with basic facilities.

Cafés

Café Alicança

Praça da República 4, Alvor ☎282 458 860. Daily 9am–2am. Opposite the turismo and next to the small Igreja Miseracórdia church, this is the locals' favourite for snacks and drinks, with outside seats on a small square.

Casa Inglêsa

Praça Manuel Teixeira Gomes, Portimão ☎282 16 290. Daily 8am–10.30pm. Large, cavernous café on the riverfront square, offering a good range of fresh juices and snacks; its sunny terrace is a popular meeting spot.

Cinco Quinas

Praia de Alvor. Daily 9am–10pm. This small beach shack, around ten minutes' walk south of Alvor's fishing harbour, attracts a young, lively clientele and offers the usual array of snacks, toasted sandwiches and grilled meat and fish.

Pastelaria Perini

Rua Dr António José D'Almeida 4, Alvor ☎282 458 144. Daily 8am–midnight. Just downhill from the tourist

office, this traditional *pastelaria* has a counter full of speciality cakes; it also offers a good range of croissants and snacks such as crepes and pizzas.

Restaurants

Bom Apetite

Rua Júdice Fialho 21, Portimão. Mon–Sat 10.30am–2am. Bargain meat and fish dishes, omelettes and jugs of house wine and sangria on a lively street full of bars and restaurants.

Casa da Maré

Largo da Ribeira 10, Alvor ☎282 458 191. Tues–Sun 10am–10pm. One of a row of slightly pricey fish restaurants on the harbourfront; this one benefits from its prime position, with tables spilling out onto the square.

La Dolce Vita

Avda Tomás Cabreira, Edifício Mar Azul, Praia da Rocha ☎282 419 444. Daily 11am–3pm & 6.30–10.30pm. A lively, inexpensive little place with rustic decor. It is owned and run by Italians, so the home-made pasta, pizzas, salads and ice creams are reliably tasty; set lunches start at €7 and there's live music at weekends.

Dockside

Marina do Portimão ☎282 417 208. Daily 10am–11pm. One of a growing number of flash modern restaurants overlook-ing the marina; this *cervejaria* and *marisqueria* serves pricey but top-quality seafood, fish and grills, including superb fish baked in salt.

Dona Barca

Largo da Barca, Portimão ☎282 484 189. Daily noon–3pm & 6–10pm. Very highly rated, expensive fish restaurant – it has frequently represented the Algarve at Lisbon's gastronomy fair – with an atmospheric interior and outdoor tables on this pretty square. Serves typical Algarve cuisine including *feijoada de Buzinas* (shellfish with beans) and regional desserts such as *tarte de amendoa* (almond tart).

Estrela do Mar

Areal da Praia da Rocha, Praia da Rocha ☎282 427 495. Daily 9am–7pm. Right on the beach with a terrace facing the sands, this simple place offers good-value fish, salads, meat dishes and ice creams. Around €15 for a full meal.

Tasca do Margadinho

Largo da Ribeirinho 9, Alvor ☎282 459 144. Mon–Wed & Fri–Sun 10am–midnight. Atmospheric *tasca* (tavern) opposite the old fish market, moderately priced, with a local feel and superbly grilled fresh fish; tables outside on the square too.

A Portuguesa

Avda Tomás Cabreira, Praia da Rocha ☎282 424 175. Mon–Sat 3pm–2am. Welcoming restaurant specializing in substantial mid-priced Portuguese grills, backed by gentle jazzy sounds most nights.

Cervejaria Praia da Rocha

Edifício Colunas, Praia da Rocha ☎282 416 514. Daily noon–3pm & 7–11pm. Tucked away in a side street opposite the casino, this bustling *cervajaria* attracts a largely local clientele thanks to good-value daily specials and well-prepared fish and grills. Around €15 for a full meal.

▲ALVOR

Restaurante Restinga

Praia de Alvor ☎282 459 434. Daily 9am–9pm. Closed one month in winter. Sitting on the cusp of a large dune, this beach bar-restaurant offers stunning views of the beach and estuary, along with decent fish meals at moderate prices.

Safari

Rua António Feu, Praia da Rocha ☎282 423 540. Daily noon–10pm. This swish restaurant overlooks the beach and serves mainly Portuguese dishes, a few with an Angolan influence. Moderate prices and attentive service.

Vô Filipe

Zona Ribeirinha, Loja 3, Portimão. Daily 10am–midnight. Best of the row of smart but inexpensive fish restaurants specializing in grilled sardines, though other fish and meat also feature.

Bars and clubs

Katedral

Avda Tomás Cabreira, Praia da Rocha June–Sept daily midnight–6am; Oct–May Thurs–Sat midnight–6am. Housed in a futuristic cube on the clifftop, this is the largest and highest-profile club in town, with a lightshow and the latest dance sounds. The downstairs bar, *Nicho*, is a good place to start the evening.

On the Rocks

Avda Tomás Cabreira, Lojas B & C, Praia da Rocha ☎282 416 144. Daily 10am–4am. A modern dance bar with a sunny terrace to catch the sunset before loud music takes hold inside. Live soccer on TV sometimes vies for attention in the bar; there's also a dance floor and live music on Fridays.

Pé de Vento

Avda Tomás Cabreira Loja A, Praia da Rocha ☎282 424 180. Daily 3pm–4am. Another popular disco bar over two floors. The upstairs bar has a beach-facing terrace next to a large dance floor that features live music on Wednesdays.

Serra de Monchique

Acting as the natural northern boundary to the Algarve, the Serra de Monchique is a delightful green and wooded mountain range of cork, chestnut and eucalyptus trees. Though frequently damaged by summer fires, the woodland is usually quick to recover and it remains ideal hiking country, embracing the region's highest peaks, Picota and Fóia. It also has one of the country's most picturesque spa resorts, Caldas de Monchique, and a small zoo.

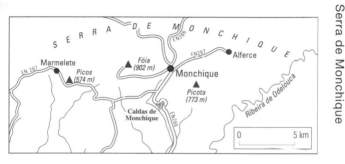

Caldas de Monchique

Caldas de Monchique, set in a steep valley and surrounded by thick woods, has been a spa since Roman times. It is particularly spectacular in autumn when the deciduous trees – a relative rarity in Portugal – display fantastic colours. In the nineteenth century the town became a favourite resort for the Spanish bourgeoisie, though these days it's coach parties that fill its main square, in high season at least. The waters are still said to have healing powers for skin and chest complaints. In recent years the whole place has been revitalized and turned into a tourist resort; old buildings have been sympathetically restored.

Halfway down the hill on the left you'll see the cobbled, tree-shaded main square, fronted by the pseudo-Moorish windows

▼MANSION, CALDAS DE MONCHIQUE

Serra de Monchique **PLACES**

Visiting Caldas de Monchique

Regular buses from Portimão pass the turning to Caldas on their way to and from Monchique. Some of these call into the centre of Caldas, though most stop instead on the main road five minutes out of town.

of the former casino – now a *pensão* – and flanked by lovely, nineteenth-century buildings. Downhill from the main square you pass the Bouvet – a little stone building where you can drink the therapeutic waters free, straight from the ground. Heading uphill, you can follow the stream out of the village to a tranquil picnic spot shaded by giant eucalyptus trees.

Caldas de Monchique spa

☎ 282 910 910, ⊛www .monchiquetermas.com. Mon 9am– 1pm, Tues 10.30am–1pm & 3–7pm, Wed–Sun 9–1pm & 3–7pm; €23. Caldas de Monchique's cutting-edge thermal spa sits downhill from the main square and offers

▼BACKSTREEETS, MONCHIQUE

various specialist water treatments on the ground floor of a modern hotel. The entrance fee gives access to the sauna, steam room, gym, water massage facilities and pool, with extra sessions ranging from forty-minute "tired leg" treatment (€25) to full body massages from €50. Discounts of twenty percent are available to hotel guests.

Omega Parque

Caldas de Monchique ☎ 282 911 327, ⊛ www.omegaparque.com. Daily: May–Sept 10am–7pm; Oct–April 10am–5.30pm. €8, children €5, family ticket €22. Set on steep wooded slopes on the road just south of Caldas de Monchique, Omega Parque is a zoo dedicated to preserving endangered species. Well cared-for residents include cheetahs, pygmy hippos and red pandas. The various birds here include the Bali starling and blue-necked cassowary, whose enclosures blend in with the natural environs. There's also a decent café and shop.

Monchique

Monchique is a small hill town whose large market on the second Friday of each month is famous for smoked hams and locally made furniture – especially distinctive x-shaped wooden chairs. Its old town, dotted with beautifully-crafted metal sculptures of local characters made by the contemporary Lisbon artist Doutor Vanancio, is a fine place for a wander. The most impressive building is the parish church, the Igreja Matriz

▲ MONASTERY OF NOSSA SENHORA DO DESTERRO, MONCHIQUE

(Mon–Sat 10am–5.30pm), up a steep cobbled street from the main square, with an imposing Manueline porch and, inside, a little chapel covered with *azulejos*.

The most evocative of the town's sights, though, is the ruined Franciscan monastery of **Nossa Senhora do Desterro**, a lovely fifteen-minute walk up through the old town. Brown signs point you eventually along a wooded track through cork and chestnut woods. Only a roofless shell of this seventeenth-century monastery survives and even that looks close to collapse. Officially it's boarded up, but locals sometimes guide you inside for a small tip.

Fóia

Buses from Monchique on Mon & Thurs (11am and 3.30pm). The 900m peak of Fóia is the highest in the Serra de Monchique. It's a lovely journey – by car or bus or an energetic walk, winding through wooded slopes dotted with upmarket inns (see pp.148–49) and *miradouros* offering superb views over the south coast. Bristling with antennae and radio masts and capped by an ungainly modern complex of a café-restaurant, shop and hotel, the summit itself can be an anticlimax, especially if clouds obscure the views or you have to share the experience with multitudes in midsummer. Get here before 10am if you can. On a clear day, however, the panoramic view of the Algarve takes in Portimão, Lagos, the foothills stretching to the Barragem da Bravura, and across west to Cabo de São Vicente.

Visiting Monchique

Buses from Portimão arrive at the terminal in the main square, Largo 5 de Outubro. Opposite here, Monchique's helpful turismo (Mon–Fri 10am–1.30pm & 2.30–6pm; ☎282 911 189) sits on a pretty pedestrianized part of the square.

▲VIEW FROM FÓIA

Picota

Reaching 770m, Picota comes second in altitude to Fóia, though it's much more interesting in terms of its flora, and easier to reach without your own transport – you can drive the 5km here, or it's a one-and-a-half-hour walk to the peak from Monchique through attractive cork plantations, fruit orchards and eucalyptus trees, with wild goats scurrying around on the higher reaches. To reach Picota, take the N266 Caldas de Monchique road, and turn left onto the N267, signposted Alferce. Picota is the second turning, signed around 800m along this road off to the right. From the top, the coastline stretches out below all the way west to Sagres, and behind is the magnificent Monchique mountain range.

Accommodation

Estalagem Abrigo da Montanha

Estrada da Fóia ☎282 912 131, ✉abrigodamontanha@hotmail.com. Just out of Monchique on the Fóia road, this modern granite and wood chalet-style inn has comfortable rooms with great views over the valley. There's also a pool, a downstairs restaurant, and a roaring fire when the air turns chilly. €87.

Pensão Central

Caldas de Monchique ☎282 910 910, ⊛www.monchiquetermas.com. Very comfortable three-star *pensão* partly set in the former casino building; modern comforts include fridges, satellite TV and a/c. €92.

Albergaria do Lageado

Caldas de Monchique. Closed Nov–April. ☎282 912 616, ☎282 911 310. Just above the main square, this lovely four-star hotel has twenty smart rooms, with TVs and en-suite bathrooms. There's a pool in the garden and an excellent restaurant. €55.

Monchique Termas apartments

Caldas de Monchique ☎282 910 910, ⊛www.monchiquetermas.com. The spa parent company hire out neat apartments overlooking the main square, with small living rooms and kitchenettes, sleeping up to four people from €100 a night.

Estrela de Monchique

Rua do Porto Fundo 46, Monchique ☎282 913 111. Just to the east of the bus terminal, this is much the best budget option in town, with bright, modern en-suite rooms; top-floor rooms have balconies. The price does not include breakfast. €35.

Estalagem de Santo António

Alto da Fóia ☎282 912 158, ☎282 912 878. Large, modern rooms with TV and baths right on the summit of Fóia – the views are superb. €60.

Quinta de São Bento

Estrada da Fóia ☎ & ☎282 912 143. Just over four kilometres out of Monchique, around 1km below the Fóia summit, this wonderful old stone *quinta* is set on a peaceful slope amongst chestnut woods. It has five comfortable rooms and one apartment and is also famed for its cuisine (see p.150). €70.

Cafés

A Nora

Largo dos Chorões, Monchique ☎282 913 750. Daily 9am–9pm. Named after the traditional well that still operates opposite, this bustling café-bar next to the turismo offers good-value snacks and light meals with tables spilling onto the attractive main square.

O Tasco

Caldas de Monchique ☎282 910 910. Daily 9am–8pm. On the far side of the main square, below the path to the picnic area, this darkened bar is housed in the oldest building in the village, in sixteenth-century stables. Specialities include bread rolls with sausagemeat baked in a traditional oven outside.

Restaurants

Restaurante 1692

Caldas de Monchique ☎282 910 910. Daily 10am–8pm. High-profile, formal and expensive restaurant named after its year of construction, with lovely outdoor tables under the trees of the main square. The menu includes interesting starters such as *morcelo* (spicy sausage), followed by conventional grilled fish and meat dishes.

Restaurante Central

Rua da Igreja 5, Monchique ☎282 913 160. Daily 11am–7.30pm. A tiny place smothered with notes and postcards detailing past visitors' comments – mainly complimentary. The menu is limited to two or three average Portuguese dishes, but the place scores high on character, and dishes are inexpensive.

▼MONCHIQUE

Restaurante A Charrete

Rua Dr. Samora Gil 30–34, Monchique ☎282 912 142. Daily 12.30–10pm. This smart restaurant on the road up to the convent is the best place to eat in Monchique, specializing in award-winning but not too pricey "mountain food" – cooked with beans, pasta and rice – along with more conventional Algarve fare. Desserts include a superb *pudim de mel* (honey pudding). Around €18 for a full meal.

Restaurante Quinta de São Bento

Estrada da Fóia ☎282 912 143. Tues–Sun noon–3pm & 7–10pm. It's worth booking ahead for a meal at this superb *quinta* (see p.149) just below Fóia. The award-winning cuisine features regional specialities, prepared with local produce such as Monchique ham, goat's cheese, *chouriço*, almonds and figs. Pricey but worth it.

O Rouxinol

Caldas de Monchique ☎282 913 975. Tues–Sun noon–10pm. Closed Dec & Jan. Highly rated restaurant set in a former hunting lodge on the main road just above town. With a giant fireplace – large enough to roast a whole pig – the inside is very cosy but there's also an outdoor terrace facing wooded slopes. The Swedish owners serve up Portuguese and international dishes, salads and great desserts. Around €15–20 for a full meal.

Lagos and around

At the mouth of the Rio Bensafrim, its historic centre enclosed in largely fourteenth-century town walls, Lagos is one of the Algarve's most attractive and historic towns. In 1577, Lagos became the administrative capital of the Algarve, and continued to thrive until much of the town was destroyed in the 1755 earthquake. Today it's a thriving resort, but it also remains a working fishing port and market centre with a life of its own. Lagos' main attraction is its proximity to some of the best beaches on the Algarve coast. To the east of the town is a long sweep of sand – Meia Praia – while to the west lies an extraordinary network of cove beaches, including Praia de Dona Ana, Praia do Pinhão and Praia do Camilo, accessible in summer on a toy train. Two different attractions lie a short drive inland: one of the Algarve's most beautiful reservoirs, the Barragem de Bravura, and Lagos Zoo, a good escape for families.

Avenida dos Descobrimentos

The palm-lined Avenida dos Descobrimentos hugs the banks of the river and offers some of the best views of the old town walls. At the *avenida*'s western stretch, the squat seventeenth-century **Forte da Ponta da Bandeira** (Tues–Sun

Visiting Lagos

Lagos is the western terminal of the Algarve rail line and its train station is fifteen minutes' walk from the town centre. The bus station (☎282 762 944) is a block back from the main Avenida dos Descobrimentos. There is free parking around the bridge to the marina on Avenida dos Descobrimentos, though you need to pay to park in the other spaces around the old town.

The turismo (May–Sept Mon–Fri 10am–7pm, Sat & Sun 10am–1pm & 2.30–6pm; Oct–April same hours until 6pm; ☎282 763 031) is at Sítio de São João, which is the first roundabout as you come into the town from the east. From the centre, it's a twenty-minute walk; keep going down Rua Vasco da Gama, past the bus station.

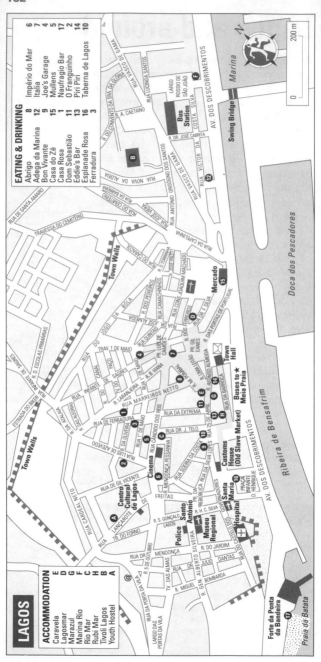

LAGOS

ACCOMMODATION

Caravela	E
Lagosmar	D
Marazul	G
Marina Rio	F
Rio Mar	C
Rubi Mar	H
Tivoli Lagos	B
Youth Hostel	A

EATING & DRINKING

Abrigo	8
Adega da Marina	12
Bon Vivante	9
Casa do Zé	15
Casa Rosa	1
Dom Sebastião	11
Eddie's Bar	13
Esplanade Rosa	16
Ferradura	3
Império do Mar	6
Italia	7
Joe's Garage	4
Mullens	5
Naufragio Bar	17
O Franguinho	2
Piri Piri	14
Taberna de Lagos	10

0   200 m

▲FORTA DA PONTA DA BANDEIRA

9.30am–12.30pm & 2–5pm; €2) guards the entrance to the harbour. The fort itself is rather uninteresting, its interior consisting of a small temporary exhibition space, though you can enjoy fine views over the water from inside. Lagos' recently renovated mercado, the bustling fruit, vegetable and fish market, also lies on the *avenida* and scores high on atmosphere.

Most days stalls set up along the *avenida*'s length offering boat trips to see the surrounding coastline (see box below), with many trips departing from the smart marina.

The marina

Backed by shops and international restaurants and filled with flash yachts, the marina can be reached by a swing bridge over the river. You can continue past it to Meia Praia (see p.155) via Lagos' characterful fishing harbour. The marina also marks the starting point of the **toy train** (May–Sept

hourly 10.30am–7pm; €3), which trundles along Avenida dos Descobrimentos and out via the beaches of Praia Dona Ana and Porto de Moz to the headland at Ponta da Piedade. The trip takes around 25 minutes one way.

The slave market and Praça da República

In one corner of the leafy Praça da República, under the arcades of the old Customs House, you'll find a sad, diminutive space that was Europe's first slave market (*mercado de escravos*). The market opened in 1444 and within a hundred years, up to 10,000 slaves were being shipped from Africa annually to meet Portuguese demand alone. Nowadays the Customs House serves as an art gallery, showing local art of dubious quality.

Opposite the slave market sits the church of **Santa Maria**, through whose windows the young king of Portugal, Dom Sebastião, is said to have roused

Boat trips

Lagos is a great place to get a boat to see the surrounding coastline. Most trips cost around €10 for a 45-minute trip, up to €17 or so for half-day sailing rides or dolphin "seafaris". The best trip is to the coastline off Ponta da Piedade (see p.156), an amazing sculpture park of pillars, caves and rock arches.

▲STATUE OF DOM SEBASTIÃO

Neoclassical town hall, but its most prominent feature is a peculiar statue of an adolescent Dom Sebastião, resembling a flowerpot man.

Museu Regional and Igreja de Santo António

Rua General, Alberto Silveira ☎282 762 301. Tues–Sun 9.30am–12.30pm & 2–5pm. €2. The Museu Regional shoehorns in just about every possible historical and quirky object relating to Lagos and the Algarve, and the random nature of the displays is all part of the appeal.

The most important items are visible on either side as you enter, including Roman remains from the dig at Boca do Rio (see p.163), featuring an amphora encrusted with coral and busts of Roman emperor Galiano, as well as an impressive wall-mounted decorative mosaic. Elsewhere, there are Neolithic axeheads, Visigothic stone coffins, jars containing misshapen animal foetuses, a display of models of Algarvian chimneys, stuffed goats, straw hats and basketry, model fishing boats, travelogues and the 1504 town charter; there are also collections of coins, medals and banknotes, sacred art, weaponry and some frightening early surgical instruments.

You exit the museum through the extraordinary interior of the neighbouring Igreja de Santo

his troops before the ill-fated Moroccan expedition of 1578, from which the king never returned.

Praça Luís de Camões and Praça Gil Eanes

From Praça da República, the narrow streets of the old town straggle east to two other attractive mosaic-paved and pedestrianized squares, Praça Luís de Camões and Praça Gil Eanes, around which you'll find Lagos' best cafés, restaurants and guesthouses. The latter square is fronted by Lagos' grand-looking

The Portuguese expeditions

Lagos played an important role in setting the Portuguese maritime explorations in motion. Gil Eanes, the first explorer to round Cape Bojador, was born in Lagos and set sail from here in 1434. Also in the fifteenth century, Henry the Navigator used the port of Lagos as a base for the new African trade. These early voyages paved the way for even greater explorations, which eventually enabled Portugal to become one of the richest countries in the world, with an empire stretching from Brazil in the west to Macau in the east.

António. Decorated around 1715, every inch of the gilt and Baroque decor is exuberantly carved, right up to and including the barrel-vaulted ceiling – representing the life of Santo António.

Meia Praia

Served by regular bus from Avenida dos Descobrimentos, or a 30min walk over the footbridge via the marina and fishing harbour. Opposite Lagos, east of the river, Meia Praia is a stunning tract of soft sand stretching 4km to the delta of the rivers Odiáxere and Arão. Flanked by the railway line and set well back from the road, the wide beach gets progressively quieter further away from town towards the greenery of the Palmares Golf Club. The beach is particularly popular with backpackers, and there are plenty of beachside cafés and restaurants along this stretch of coastline

Praia da Batata

Despite being right on the edge of town, just beyond the Forte Ponta da Bandeira, Praia da Batata (Potato Beach) is an alluring stretch of sand, reached through a natural rock tunnel. In late August, the town beach is the venue for the Banho festival, an annual beach party marking the end of summer, with evening barbecues, live music and a traditional midnight swim.

Praia do Pinhão

Praia do Pinhão is the first of the cove beaches tucked into the promontory south of Lagos. It is a lovely, sheltered, sandy bay beneath steep cliffs. It is around fifteen minutes' walk from Lagos – follow Avenida dos Descobrimentos up the hill (toward Sagres) and it's signed left just opposite the fire station.

Praia de Dona Ana

Out of season at least, Praia de Dona Ana is one of the most photogenic of all the Algarve's beaches, a wide expanse of sand framed by cliffs, weirdly sculpted rock pillars and caves. However, the cliffs above it are lined with cafés, hotels and apartments, and in high season the sands are heaving. You can walk here along the clifftop path from Praia do Pinhão; the beach can also be reached from Lagos on the seasonal toy train (see p.153).

Praia do Camilo

Praia do Camilo is another fine beach backed by natural rock art, and being a bit further from Lagos tends to be less crowded. It is well signed off

▼FALLING FOR THE CLIFF-BACKED COVE BEACHES

the coast road and can also be reached by the toy train (see p.153).

Ponta da Piedade

Tall palms and a handsome lighthouse mark the craggy headland of Ponta da Piedade, a great vantage point for the sunset. It has a similar, if less desolate air, to Cabo de São Vicente with sweeping views down the coast as well as a handy café. This is also the final port of call for the toy train from Lagos (see p.153).

A popular coastal path from Ponta da Piedade continues as far as Luz (see p.161), an exhilarating hour and forty-five minutes' walk away.

▲LIGHTHOUSE AT PONTA DA PIEDADE

Barragem de Bravura

The Barragem de Bravura is one of the most picturesque of the Algarve's several *barragens* (reservoirs), plugged by a huge dam over the river Bravura. To the south of the dam, the deep valley is little more than an overgrown stream fed by a waterfall from the dam, while behind the dam lie the deep, still green waters of the reservoir, stirred by basking carp. It's an idyllic spot, and you can walk right over the top of the dam and round the edges of the reservoir on the other side along a dirt trail. Swimming, fishing and water sports, however, are prohibited.

There is no public transport to the Barragem de Bravura, but with your own transport it is a lovely seventeen-kilometre drive from Lagos through unspoilt countryside.

▼THE DAM AT BARRAGEM DE BRAVURA

Lagos Zoo

Quinta Figueiros, Barão de São João
☎ 282 680 100, ⊛ www.zoolagos
.com. Daily: May–Sept 10am–7pm;
Oct–April 10am-5pm. €8, children
€5, family ticket €21. Lagos Zoo
makes an enjoyable diversion
for families. Set in thirty square
kilometres of land, the well-
tended zoo is keen to publicize
its environmental awareness, and
the various birds including flamingos, toucans, ibis, parrots and
emus, as well as a few mammals
such as wallabies and monkeys,
certainly seem as happy as can
be expected. There are also farm
animals in a special children's
enclosure that children can pet
and help feed. There's a shop,
a decent restaurant, and a children's playground.

Accommodation

Pensão Caravela

Rua 25 de Abril 16, Lagos ☎ 282
763 361. In a great position
right on the old town's main
pedestrianized street, the rooms
here are clean but pretty basic.
Doubles come with or without
bath. Price includes breakfast.
€40.

Pensão Dona Ana

Praia de Dona Ana ☎ 282 762 322.
This small, white *pensão* on the
cliffs above Praia de Dona Ana
has twenty simple, clean rooms,
although the views are largely
blocked by the neighbouring
Sol e Praia. €35.

Pensão Lagosmar

Rua Dr. Faria e Silva 13, Lagos ☎ 282
763 523, ⊛ dfhoteis@inoxnet.com.
Upmarket *pensão*, with spotless
rooms mostly facing a quiet side
street. All rooms have TVs and
private bathrooms while some
also have small balconies. Off-

season rates are virtually half
those of high season. €74.

Residencial Marazul

Rua 25 de Abril 13, Lagos ☎ 282 770
230, ⊛ pensaomarazul.hotmail
.com. Closed Dec–March. Beautifully
decorated *residencial*, with bright
rooms and communal areas tiled
in *azulejos*. En-suite bedrooms
vary in size, but all come with
TVs and some have terraces
with sea views. €53.

Albergaria Marina Rio

Avda dos Descobrimentos 388, Lagos
☎ 282 769 859, ⊛ www.marinario
.com. Ungainly, large modern
inn offering decent rooms plus
satellite TV, a games room and
a rooftop pool. Front rooms
face the harbour across the busy
avenida (back rooms face the bus
station). €93.

Hotel Rio Mar

Rua Cândido dos Reis 83, Lagos
☎ 282 763 091, ☎ 282 763 927.
Smart, medium-sized hotel
with its own bar, tucked into a
central street. Most rooms have
a balcony – the best overlook
the sea at the back of the hotel,
others overlook a fairly quiet
main street. €60.

Pensão Rubi Mar

Rua da Barroca 70–1°, Lagos ☎ 282
763 165, ⊛ rubimar01@hotmail.com.
A wonderful old *pensão* with
spacious rooms, most en suite
and some with balconies, the
best with harbour views. Also
has rooms sleeping up to five,
and the price includes breakfast.
€45.

Apartamentos Marvela

Rua Dr. José Formosinho, Praia do
Pinhão ☎ & ☎ 282 760 600. On the
road above Praia do Pinhão,
these good-value apartments
sleep up to three people and

come with a small kitchenette and balcony or terrace. €80.

Meia Praia Beach Club

Meia Praia ☎282 789 400, ⊕www .dompedro.com. Around ten minutes' drive out of Lagos, just back from one of the best stretches of beach, this tasteful three-star is set in attractive grounds; the best rooms have sea-facing balconies. Apartments for 4–6 people are also on offer. There are tennis courts, a pool, and guests are entitled to discounts at the Palmares Golf Course (see p.191). €115.

Sol e Praia

Praia de Dona Ana ☎282 762 026, ⊕282 760 247. The newest and best option on this stretch of coast – close to the steps down to the beach and with facilities including a pool, gym and games room. The rooms aren't huge but are comfortable, and many have sea-facing balconies which cost €8 extra. €73.

Tivoli Lagos

Rua Nova da Aldeia, Lagos ☎282 790 079, ⊕www.tivolilagos.com. Lagos' most upmarket central hotel is built "village-style" with paths linking rooms, a restaurant, indoor and outdoor pool and health club. There's a courtesy bus to its own beach club at Meia Praia, but the rooms aren't huge and some overlook a busy street. €160.

Youth hostel

Rua de Lançarote de Freitas 50, Lagos ☎282 761 970, ⊕lagos@movijovem .pt. A modern, well-designed youth hostel, just up from the Centro Cultural de Lagos, with several dorms (€15) plus a few en-suite doubles (€45); be sure to book in advance. There's a nice central courtyard plus Internet access and currency exchange.

Campsite

Parque de Campismo da Trindade

Rossio da Trindade ☎282 763 893, ⊕282 762 885. A basic, cramped campsite with a small shop, on the way to Praia de Dona Ana. In season, a bus marked "D. Ana/Porto de Mós" runs to the site from the bus station. On foot, it's about ten to fifteen minutes from the Forte Ponta da Bandeira. A taxi from the centre costs around €5.

Cafés

Cervejaria Abrigo

Rua Marquês de Pombal 2, Lagos. Mon–Sat 8.30am–9.30pm. With outdoor tables in a little square under scented orange trees, this aromatic café makes a great breakfast stop, with fluffy fresh croissants; also serves beer, cocktails, snacks and meals all day.

Esplanade Rosa

Praça Infante D. Henrique, Lagos. Daily 9am–2am. This kiosk opposite the Igreja Santa Maria has outdoor tables sprawling across the leafy square adjacent to Praça da República. Serves inexpensive pastries, pizzas, coffees and beer.

Gaivota Branca

Meia Praia. Daily 10am–midnight. The perfect beachside café, set just over the railway lines on an idyllic stretch of beach opposite the *Dom Pedro Hotel*. The "white seagull" serves the usual range of snacks and seafood as well as drinks.

A Recanto da Barragem

Barragem de Bravura. April–Oct
Tues–Sun 10am–6pm. A few
hundred metres from the car
park near the reservoir, this
seasonal café serves drinks and
decent snacks inside or on
an outdoor terrace next to a
small children's playground.

Restaurants

Adega da Marina

Avda dos Descobrimentos 35, Lagos
⊕282 764 284. Daily noon–2am. Set
in a former warehouse, this
great barn of a place serves
excellent food at tables lined
up as if for a wedding party.
Huge portions of good value
charcoal-grilled meat and fish
plus great house wines. Full
meals for around €12.

Casa do Zé

Avda dos Descobrimentos, Lagos.
Daily 6am–2am. A tiny bar-restaurant next to the market, with
outside seats facing the harbour
offering filling dishes – mostly
fish but some meat – from an
inexpensive menu chalked up
on the board.

Casa Rosa

Rua do Ferrador 22, Lagos. Tues–Sun
noon–3pm & 6–11pm. Bar-restaurant that bills itself as a
"backpacker's paradise". Set
meals start at €5 and other
dishes – ranging from stir fries
and chocolate muffins to Portuguese staples – are good value
too. Drinking begins in earnest
with a 7pm happy hour.

Dom Sebastião

Rua 25 de Abril 20–22, Lagos ⊕282
762 795. Daily noon–3pm & 6–11pm.
Arguably the town's finest restaurant, with outdoor seating
and a traditional cobbled inte-

▲PEDESTRIANIZED STREETS, LAGOS OLD TOWN

rior. Serves good seafood and a
fabulous selection of appetizers
and reasonable vegetarian dishes,
though meat dishes can be dis-
appointing. A full fish meal runs
to about €20.

O Franguinho

Rua Luís de Azevedo 25, Lagos.
Tues–Sun 11am–2.30pm & 5.30–
10.30pm. Bustling, good-value
churrasqueria with a tiny, first-
floor dining room. This is the
place to go for fine (if greasy)
chicken or *febras de porco* (grilled
pork steaks). There are daily
changing specials. Around €12
for a full meal.

Italia

Rua Garrett 26–28, off Praça Luís
Camões, Lagos ⊕282 760 030. Daily
noon–3pm & 6.30–11pm. Bright,
cheery restaurant run by Italians offering moderately priced

pasta, pizzas cooked in a wood-burning oven, Italian wine, and a full menu besides. There are a few tables outside on the busy square.

Cervejaria Mirante

Praia de Dona Ana. Daily 9am–midnight. Right on the cliff overlooking the sands, this is a great place to enjoy the house specialities such as *espetada de tamboril* (monkfish kebab) and *norvilho na brasa* (chargrilled steaks). Also does moderately priced pizzas, snacks and a range of drinks.

Piri Piri

Rua Afonso Almeida 10, Lagos ☎282 763 803. Daily noon–3pm & 7pm–2am. Simple place on the main pedestrianized street serving filling grills, though the best bet is the superb chicken piri-piri for only around €5.

Bars and clubs

Bon Vivante

Rua 25 Abril 105, Lagos. Daily 10pm–4am. Just north of the old slave market, this late-night disco bar has gaudy marble pillars and a superb "tropical" roof terrace; a good place to hit when the other bars have closed.

Eddie's Bar

Rua 25 de Abril 99, Lagos ☎282 768 329. Daily 4pm–2am. Small, dark-wood bar with a good selection of sounds and attracting a friendly, surf-dude kind of crowd.

Cervejaria Ferradura

Rua 1° de Maio 269, Lagos. Mon–Sat 10am–2am. An atmospheric *cervejaria* – very much a locals' place – with walls covered in soccer posters and stacks of inexpensive petiscos on the bar.

Império do Mar

Rua Cândido dos Reis 119, Lagos. Mon–Sat 10am–4am, Sun 2pm–4am. Lively bar with ranks of Internet terminals, TV screens for big soccer games and bar snacks including pizzas and sandwiches. Attracts a youthful clientele.

Joe's Garage

Rua I° de Maio 78, Lagos. Daily 7pm–2am. Disco bar that's thronging with Antipodeans drinking heavily and dancing on the tables. A filling plate of food costs €5; you know it's closing time when they set fire to the bar.

Mullens

Rua Cândido dos Reis 86, Lagos ☎282 761 281. Daily 8pm–2am. This atmospheric, cavernous *adega* is the most appealing late-night choice in town. Inexpensive drinks including Guinness, sangria and *vinho verde* on tap are served alongside excellent and moderately priced meals to a jazz and soul soundtrack.

Naufragio Bar

Avda dos Descobrimentos, Lagos. Daily 10am–2am. Pleasant beach bar with a youthful clientele, jazzy sounds and moderately priced bar snacks. Out the back there's a great terrace facing the town beach and the Forte da Ponta da Bandeira.

Taberna de Lagos

Rua 25 de Abril, Lagos ☎282 084 250. Daily 10am–10pm. Lovely, high-ceilinged town house converted into a sophisticated wine bar-restaurant that attracts a laid-back, arty crowd. Superb cocktails include caipirinhas and alcohol-free fruit cocktails, and bar snacks include mid-priced pizza, pasta and salads.

The southwest coast

The southwest Algarve is less built up than the central stretch, the lush Mediterranean-type vegetation giving way to coarser Atlantic scrub and grassland. It's a highly scenic area of gently rolling hills, clifftop walks and remote coves. The coast has just three resorts, of which Luz is the most upmarket. Neighbouring Burgau marks the eastern boundary of the Parque Natural do Sudoeste Alentejano e Costa Vicentina, a natural park set up to protect the coast from further development. Bustling in summer, Burgau and neighbouring Salema retain vestiges of their former status as fishing villages while nearby, you can still find quiet isolated beaches largely devoid of tourists around Figueira, Raposeira and Vila do Bispo.

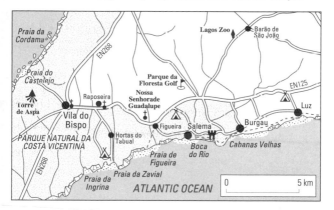

Luz

Around six daily buses from Lagos. With a wide crescent of sandy beach towered over by high cliffs, the village of Luz is beautifully situated if devoid of any real centre. White chalets and villas cluster behind the beach, but the development is generally low-key and low-rise. Buses from Lagos drop you at the edge of the old village, from where it's a short walk downhill to the attractive palm-lined beachside promenade, lined with cafés, restaurants and souvenir stalls. Between May and September its

▼LUZ SEAFRONT PROMENADE

Luz coastal walks

There are some excellent local coast walks within easy reach of Luz. The easiest of these is to the triangulation point obelisk (*atalaia*) on the clifftop to the east of Luz, a forty-minute round trip which offers great views down the coast. To get there, follow the road that runs parallel to the beach eastwards. At the edge of town you'll see a cobbled track in front of you. Take this, turning left away from the shore at a fork. The track becomes a dirt path as you head up a very steep hillside towards the obelisk, clearly visible ahead of you. If you want to walk further, you can continue along the coast path from here all the way to Porto de Mós (1hr) and Lagos (a further 45min), an exhilarating and breezy clifftop walk with striking views towards Ponta da Piedade (see p.156), though it becomes increasingly built up from Porto de Mós on.

A shorter but equally bracing walk from Luz is to head west along the coast path to Burgau (1hr). From the beachside promenade pass the fort and take the first left, continuing straight on until the road turns into a track. You'll pick up the coast path on the left after around ten minutes. The track runs parallel to the coast until you reach Burgau, offering more superb views over the sea and back towards town.

proximity to Lagos means the beach gets packed, especially at weekends. Outside summer the beach is quiet, with just a few ex-pats walking their dogs, and most of its beachside restaurants close down. Swimming is best at the western end of the sands; the other end, below the dramatic cliffs, becomes more rocky. An attractive palm-lined promenade passes from the beach above a rocky foreshore to the town's unobtrusive church and an old fort, now a restaurant (see p.168).

Luz is a popular base for sports enthusiasts; facilities at the plush *Luz Bay Club* (☎282 789 640, day membership is €11), just south of the main road from Lagos, include a sauna and pool plus tennis, squash and wall tennis.

Burgau

Around six daily buses from Lagos. With narrow cobbled lanes tumbling down a steep hillside to a fine sandy beach, Burgau is a handsome little resort where fishermen still work.

▼BURGAU

▲ BURGAU BEACH

Their colourful boats line the lower roads, which double up as slipways, while the upper roads weave around the coastline to a clifftop *miradouro* offering fine views over the sands. The beach, set below low cliffs, gets busy in high season, but for much of the year the town is delightfully tranquil.

The road into Burgau passes the Burgau Sports Centre (☎282 697 350), a well-equipped sports centre with a gym, tennis, squash, swimming pool and a kids' playground; there's also a bar and restaurant.

Boca do Rio

Set below the ruins of a seventeenth-century fortress in a broad, flat river valley, Boca do Rio ("mouth of the river") is an unspoilt bay strewn with giant boulders. Once this was an important Roman settlement, and many of the remains at Lagos' Museu Regional were found at this spot. The bay is a popular spot for campervanners, and at low tide sands are revealed, making it a decent swimming spot.

Parque da Floresta

Just off the EN125, by the village of Budens, you'll see the extensive grounds of the Parque da Floresta (☎282 690 007, ⓦ www.vigiasa.com), a huge sports centre and holiday village complex set round the western Algarve's main golf course and boasting a pool, spa, tennis courts, restaurants and kids' entertainment programme.

Burgau–Salema walk

You can walk to Salema from Burgau (1hr 30min) along a bracing clifftop coastal path, which begins west of Burgau. There are great views back up the coast towards Lagos and you can stop off at a series of remote bays, including Cabanas Velhas and Boca do Rio (see above). The coast path eventually joins the road winding down to Salema.

Salema

Six to eight daily buses from Lagos and Sagres. Approached down a delightful, cultivated valley, the small fishing village of Salema has a long stretch of beach and a low-key charm that makes it popular with independent travellers. Buses stop just above the beach, where brightly coloured boats are still hauled up for the day. The atmospheric old centre spreads east from the bus stop parallel to the beach, a network of narrow alleys and white-washed fishermen's houses, many now given over to inexpensive holiday lets: just stroll round and look for the signs, or ask at the local bars if you want to stay.

Figueira and Praia da Figueira

Regular buses from Lagos and Sagres; some stop on the main EN125, a short walk from Figueira. To get to appreciate some of the unspoilt coastal countryside of the south-west Algarve, one of the best easy walks is to take the path to the beach of Praia da Figueira. This is a fine bay – often deserted except for a few naturists – with the sparse remains of a fort on the hill above. The delightful 25-minute walk starts in Figueira, a small agricultural village whose surrounding fields are still tilled by mules. Signed Forte da Figueira, the track heads down beside a river through farmland, passing traditional wells. The path narrows, following a narrow river over-grown with wild thyme and fennel. To get to the beach, cross the shallow stream at the end.

Nossa Senhora de Guadalupe

Between Figueira and Rapo-seira, a sign points off the main EN125 to the chapel of Nossa Senhora de Guadalupe, a squat, dark-stoned church reached down the old road which runs parallel to the highway. Built in the thirteenth century by the Knights Templar and said to have been frequented by Henry the Navigator, the chapel stands in rural solitude. It is usually kept locked, but it's a pleasant place to stroll around or have a picnic.

▼SALEMA BEACH

▲VILA DO BISPO

Raposeira, Praia do Zavial and Praia da Ingrina

Henry the Navigator is believed to have lived for a while in the small rural village of Raposeira, an attractive enough place with a handsome church. However, the village is sliced through by the speeding highway, and there's not much reason to come here except to turn off the road to a couple of fine beaches. Praia do Zavial is a fine, small, rock-and-sand bay below low cliffs, a popular spot with surfers thanks to its large breakers. For better swimming in a more sheltered spot, continue down the road another kilometre round the bay to Praia da Ingrina, a small sandy cove, good for beachcombing amid the rock pools.

Vila do Bispo

Vila do Bispo is a fairly traditional if rundown Algarve village with a core of old white houses. It is centred on a lovely seventeenth-century parish church (Mon–Sat 10am–1pm & 2–6pm), every interior surface of which has been painted, tiled or gilded. In September the town holds a highly atmospheric agricultural expo, where crusty farm folk enjoy food stalls and music; at other times it is quiet with no other sights, but it makes a pleasant spot for a coffee or a meal in one of the bars and restaurants before moving on to one of the nearby beaches.

Praia do Castelejo

One of the area's best beaches is Praia do Castelejo, reached via Vila do Bispo – from the main square, take the road downhill past the post office, turn left and then bear right – along a narrow road leading 5km west. It crosses a stretch of bleak moors and hills, the final approach down a winding and precipitous descent. But it is worth the effort: the beach is a huge swathe of sand (which can be covered in high tides) lashed by heavy waves below dark grey cliffs. The beach has an edge-of-the-world feel, though the beachside café adds a slight touch of civilization.

▲PRAIA DE CASTELEJO

Accommodation

Hotel Belavista da Luz

Urbanização da Belavista, Luz ☎282 788 655, ⓔhoteldaluz@mail.telepac .pt. Around 1km uphill on the road towards Sagres, this pink, modern four-star lacks character but is the best option for comfort, complete with all mod cons including a restaurant and pool. Disabled access. €150.

Casa Grande

Burgau ☎282 697 416, ⓔcasagrande@mail.telepac.pt. At the northeastern point of town on the road towards Luz, this beautiful, English-run manor house is set in its own grounds and fronted by a spiky dragon tree. There are giant rooms with soaring ceilings, each decorated with a motley assortment of period furniture. Upstairs rooms are largest with their own balconies (€80). Book ahead in high season as there are only a handful of rooms. €40.

Estalagem Infante do Mar

Salema ☎282 690 100, ⓦwww .infantedomar.com. Around 1km from Salema – steeply uphill on the road to Figueira – this smart four-star inn has comfortable rooms with panoramic views. All mod cons including a restaurant, bar and pool. €85.

Luz Bay Club

Rua do Jardim, Luz ☎282 789 640, ⓦwww.lunahoteis.com. Sports club which also rents out high-standard apartments round the town, from studios for two people to two-bed apartments sleeping up to four. All come with kitchenettes, TVs and balconies, some of which have sea views. Studios €115, apartments €130.

A Mare

Salema ☎282 695 165, ⓔjohnmare@mail.telepac.pt. On the hill above the main road into town, this good-value and attractively renovated house has a lovely sea-facing terrace and an airy breakfast room. En-suite rooms are tiny but spotless. €60.

Hotel Praia do Burgau

Burgau ☎282 690 160, ⓔdfhoteis @inoxnet.com. On a hillside to the east of town, this modern three-star has decent rooms with their own mini bars and satellite TV. The top rooms (€15 extra) have balconies with superb views, and there's also a small pool. €102.

Hotel Residencial Salema

Rua 28 de Janeiro, Salema ☎282 665 328, ⓔhotel.salema@clix.pt. Closed Nov–Feb. Plonked rather unceremoniously by the cobbled square just back from the beach, this modern block offers decent accommodation in small rooms, some with their own balconies with skewed sea views. There's also a bar and TV room. €87.

Campsites

Parque de Campismo da Quinta dos Carriços

Quinta dos Carriços, Salema ☎282 695 201, ✉quintacarrico@oninet.pt. Excellent campsite with landscaped grounds, beautifully positioned 1.5km from Salema up towards the main highway – the bus passes on the way into the village. It's well equipped with a mini market, restaurant, bar, launderette and even a car wash.

Parque de Campismo da Praia da Ingrina

Praia da Ingrina ☎ & ☎282 639 242. Around 1km inland from Praia da Ingrina, this basic campsite sits in a lovely rural setting. Limited facilities include a small shop and an attractive bar-restaurant.

Camping Valverde

Luz ☎282 789 211; advance bookings ☎218 117 070, ✇www.orbitur.pt . An attractive leafy campsite 1.5km from Luz. Close to the highway, with a full range of tourist facilities including a kids' playground, restaurant, supermarket and bar.

Cafés

Convivio

Praça da República, Vila do Bispo. Daily 10am–2am. With tables outside on the central square by the church, this is an enjoyable place to have a light meal or coffee. Also does a lethal range of cocktails.

Kiwi Pastelaria

Avenida dos Pescadores, Luz Daily 9am–10pm. Right on the beachside promenade, the outdoor tables offer an ideal breakfast stop, with fresh croissants, fruit juices and coffee. Also serves a good range of ice creams, salads and sandwiches.

Restaurants

Adega Casa Grande

Burgau ☎282 697 416. March–Oct Mon–Fri 7–11pm. Attached to the *Casa Grande* guesthouse (see p.166), this bar-restaurant is set in a former wine cellar (*adega*). It offers great, inexpensive Portuguese grills and international dishes such as chicken curry; there are also vegetarian options.

A Barraca

Largo dos Pescadores 2, Burgau ☎282 697 748. Daily noon–3pm & 7–10pm. This clifftop restaurant is a top spot for mid-priced meat dishes and seafood, including the speciality, *cataplanas*. It's best in summer as, at other times, plastic sheets over the terrace put paid to the wind but also the views.

Beach Bar Burgau

Praia de Burgau ☎282 697 553. Restaurant: Tues–Sun noon–3pm & 7–10pm; bar: April–Oct Mon 9.30am–7pm, Tues–Sun 9.30am–2am; Nov–March Tues–Sun noon–3pm. Restaurant-bar with a splendid terrace on the beach, around which the waves crash at high tide. It's best to reserve to be guaranteed an evening table. The fish and grills are slightly pricey but well presented. Alternatively, enjoy a beer or five at its late-opening bar.

Boia Bar Restaurante

Rua das Pescadores 101, Salema ☎282 695 382. Daily 10.30am–2am. On the edge of the old centre, this smart, modern restaurant does a good range of tasty if pricey fish; the superb *caldeirada* (fish stew) for four is the speciality.

Restaurante Correia

Rua 1º de Maio, Vila do Bispo. Mon–Fri & Sun 1–3pm & 7–10pm. Just down from the church, this attractive, roomy restaurant has *azulejos* on the walls and a good-value menu of grilled meats and fish (meals around €12).

Fortaleza da Luz

Rua da Igreja 3, Luz ☎282 789 926. Daily noon–3pm & 7–9.30pm. The Fortaleza (castle) is the most upmarket choice in Luz, with pricey top-notch pasta dishes, omelettes and Algarvian dishes, such as pork Monchique-style and delicious *bolo de amendôa* (almond cake). There are tables on the grassy terrace and its ornate dining room offers superb sea views; there's also occasional live music at weekends.

Mira Mar

Travessa Mira Mar 6, Salema ☎919 560 339. Daily 12.30–3pm & 7–11pm. Small, simple but very welcoming restaurant right on the beach. Excellent and well-priced fresh fish – the bream is superb – is served on a little terrace facing the waves. The house wine is good value too. Around €15 a full meal.

O Poço

Avda dos Pescadores, Luz. Daily 12.30–3pm & 7–10pm. "The well" boasts a prime spot overlooking the sands and the beachside promenade. The reasonably priced seafood and meat dishes include an excellent *espadarte de tamboril* (monkfish kebab), and the service is snappy.

Restaurante Praia do Castelejo

Praia do Castelejo ☎282 639 777. May–Sept Mon, Tues & Thurs–Sun 10.30am–8pm. Welcoming café-restaurant supplying drinks, snacks and the usual, mid-priced Portuguese fare including *cataplanas* on a terrace facing the sands.

Sebastião

Praia da Ingrina. Mon & Wed–Sun 11am–10pm. A little stone beachside café-restaurant where you can tuck into filling grills (around €15) or enjoy drinks on a palm-shaded terrace facing the waves.

Restaurante Zavial

Praia do Zavial. Tues–Sun noon–5pm & 7–10pm ☎282 639 282. Set in a modern stone building with a beach-facing terrace, this beach restaurant serves a decent range of moderately priced and tasty grilled meat and fish. There's also inexpensive baguettes and a special kids' menu.

Bars

Bar Aventura

Rua das Pescadores 80, Salema ☎282 695 663, Daily 9am–2am. Attractive French-owned bar on the road into the old village, attracting a young crowd. It also offers Internet access (€4.50/hr).

Bar Brizze

Rua 25 Abril, Burgau ☎963 319 845. Daily 8am–midnight. Small bar with a series of outdoor terraces on Burgau's steepest beachside approach. It's a great stop for a morning coffee and croissant or an evening beer.

The Bull

Rua da Calheta 2, Luz. Daily 11am–2am. Just up from the fort, this English-style pub has a range of drinks, English breakfasts and inexpensive pub grub firmly geared to British tastes. There's an outdoor terrace, but it's liveliest when everyone crams inside for the latest soccer game on TV.

Sagres and around

Teetering on the edge of the continent, Sagres is the most southwesterly harbour in Europe. It spreads along a clifftop above a working fishing harbour, and although it is a straggling, ungainly town, its dramatic position and proximity to superb beaches attracts substantial summer crowds. At other times it's popular with surfers, lured by superb waves and four local surf schools. Numerous day-trippers also pass through here to see Cabo de São Vicente, a dramatic lighthouse-capped headland, and the imposing fortress, believed to be Prince Henry the Navigator's school of navigation. On 15 August – Sagres' lively Saint's Day – the town celebrates with music, dancing and fireworks.

Praça da República

Praça da República is the main focus of the town, an attractive cobbled space lined with squat palms and whitewashed cafés. At the end of the day, the elderly gather at the dusty square alongside the tourist office to play animated games of boules.

The mercado

North of the square, Sagres' mercado (market) on Rua do Mercado (Mon–Sat 8am–1pm) sells superb fresh fruit and vegetables as well as a section for fish. On the first Friday of each month, the area around the market building forms the venue for a lively regional flea market.

The Fortaleza

Daily: May–Sept 10am–8.30pm; Oct–April 10am–6.30pm. €3, students €1.20. The white walls of Sagres' Fortaleza (fortress) dominate the

▲IGREJA DE NOSSA SENHORA DA GRAÇA IN
THE FORTALEZA

clifftops southwest of the village.
An immense circuit of walls
once surrounded this vast, shelf-
like promontory, high above the
Atlantic. But what you see today
was largely rebuilt in 1793: only
the north side survives intact,
the rest destroyed in the 1755
earthquake.

The entrance is through a
formidable rock tunnel, before
which is spread a huge pebble
wind compass known as the
Rosa dos Ventos (wind rose),
unearthed beneath a church in
1921 and used to measure the
direction of the wind. Its 43-
metre diameter is divided into
forty low segments made of
stone, radiating out like a bike
wheel. No one is sure whether
the compass dates back to
Henry's time, though the simple,
much-restored chapel of **Nossa
Senhora da Graça** beside the
compass is accepted as dating
from the fifteenth century.

Over the last few years some
new buildings have appeared
within the fortress walls – a
shop, café and exhibition space
showing maps of Portugal and
other nautical memorabilia –
but, gracelessly constructed with
concrete, they've done little to
enhance the beauty of the site.
However, it's lovely to wander
around the walls and out to
Ponta de Sagres, a headland with
a small lighthouse beacon offering fine views up and down the
coast, past precariously balanced
fishermen dangling their lines
off the immense cliffs.

Praia da Mareta and Praia de Tonel

Most of Sagres' excellent beaches
are within easy walking distance
of the town. The nearest (and
therefore most crowded) beach,
Praia da Mareta, is a lovely

Prince Henry's School of Navigation

Henry developed thirteenth-century fortifications at Sagres to form a secure base
for his seafaring academy, and spent the last three years of his life working in the
Fortaleza from his home in Sagres. Here, the Prince gathered some of the great-
est astronomers, cartographers and adventurers of his age. Fernão de Magalhães
(Magellan), Pedro Álvares Cabral and Vasco da Gama all studied at Sagres, and
from the beach at Beliche – midway between the capes of Sagres and São Vicente
– the first caravels were launched, thus revolutionizing shipping with their wide
hulls, small adaptable sails, and ability to sail close to the wind. Each year new
expeditions were dispatched to penetrate a little further into the unknown, and
to resolve the great navigational enigma presented by the west coast of Africa,
thereby laying the foundations of the country's overseas empire.

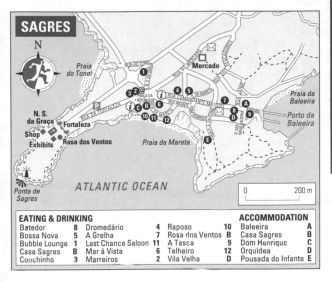

SAGRES

N

Praia do Tonel

Mercado

RUA DO TONEL

RUA DA FORTALEZA

RUA COMANDANTE MATOSO

PRAÇA DA REPÚBLICA

RUA INFANTE

N.S. da Graça

Fortaleza

Shop
Exhibits
Rosa dos Ventos

Praia da Mareta

Praia da Baleeira

Porto da Baleeira

R. DAS
NAUS BALEEIRA

ATLANTIC OCEAN

Ponta de Sagres

0   200 m

EATING & DRINKING				ACCOMMODATION	
Batedor	8	Dromedário	4	Raposo	10	Baleeira	A
Bossa Nova	5	A Grelha	7	Rosa dos Ventos	B	Casa Sagres	B
Bubble Lounge	1	Last Chance Saloon	11	A Tasca	9	Dom Henrique	C
Casa Sagres	B	Mar á Vista	6	Telheiro	12	Orquídea	D
Conchinha	3	Marreiros	2	Vila Velha	D	Pousada do Infante	E

stretch of soft sand just five to ten minutes' walk downhill southeast from Praça da República. Out towards the fortress, Praia de Tonel is another superb sandy beach below cliffs, popular with surfers: take great care when swimming as the undertow can be fierce.

Porto da Baleeira and Praia do Martinhal

Sagres' atmospheric Porto da Baleeira ("port of the whale-boats") is very much a working harbour, lined with fishing boats and boat-building yards: this is also where you can arrange boat trips or diving courses. You can squeeze past the slipways and boatyard debris onto Praia da Baleeira, another fine, if diminutive, sandy beach. For space, however, you're better off continuing east for five to ten minutes along the clifftop above the harbour to Praia do Martinhal, a wide sandy crescent that is generally quieter than the other beaches, backed by beachside

cafés, a marshy lagoon and complete with a windsurfing school (☎282 624 147), which can also organize kite surfing.

▼LOBSTER POTS, PORTO DA BALEEIRA

▲WINDSURFERS, PRAIA DO MARTINHAL

Praia de Beliche

Out on the road to Cabo de São Vicente, with correspondingly fewer crowds, Praia de Beliche is where Henry the Navigator's caravels first set off to explore the unknown world; little can have changed here since, and you are usually guaranteed plenty of sand to yourself. The beach, set beneath steep cliffs, is overlooked by a small fortress, once a restaurant and *pousada*, but currently closed for safety reasons.

Cabo de São Vicente

The wild headland of Cabo de São Vicente is the most south-westerly point of the Iberian peninsula. Known as Promontorium Sacrum, the headland was sacred to the Romans, who believed the sun sank hissing into the water beyond here every night. Legend has it that in the eighth century, Christians took the remains of Saint Vincent with them from Spain to flee invading Moors, arriving at the safe outpost of the cape, where they later built a chapel to house his bones, though these were later moved to Lisbon.

Today the only buildings to be seen are the ruins of a sixteenth-century Capuchin monastery and a nineteenth-century light-house, which has the most powerful beam in Europe. The cape is a dramatic and exhilarating six-kilometre walk from Sagres, with a cliff path skirting the vertiginous drop for much of the way. Walking on the road is easier if slightly less scenic – it'll take less than an hour and a half, with glorious views all the way. Try to be at the cape for sunset, which is invariably gorgeous, though frequently very windy too. Today the sea off this wild set of cliffs shelters the highest concentration of marine life in Portugal, and it is also rich in birdlife: at various times of year you should be able to spot blue rock thrushes and peregrine falcons nesting on the cliffs along with rare birds such as Bonelli's eagles, white storks, rock doves, kites and white herons.

Accommodation

Hotel da Baleeira

Porto da Baleeira, Sagres ☎282 624 212, ⊚www.sagres.net/baleeira. This modern hotel has sweeping harbour views, a large pool and tennis courts. Rooms are spacious and comfortable with TVs and en-suite facilities, though you pay €15 extra for views. €112.

Casa Sagres

Praça da República, Sagres ☎282 624 358. Behind the main square on the road down to Praia da Mareta, this is primarily a restaurant (see p.174) that also lets out decent en-suite rooms. The best ones have sea-facing balconies (€5 extra). €65.

Residencial Dom Henrique

Praça da República, Sagres ☎282 620 000, ☎282 620 001. In a perfect position on the main square and with a terrace offering wonderful sea views, this is a good first port of call. There's an airy bar and rooms have bath and satellite TV; rooms with sea-facing balconies €85, otherwise €78.

Motel Gambozinhos

Praia do Martinhal, Apt.14 ☎282 620 160, ☎282 620 169. Attractively located, simple motel with a line of rooms and apartments set in peaceful gardens just back from the sands of Praia do Martinhal. Two-bed apartments start at €65.

Aparthotel Orquídea

Sítio da Baleeira, Sagres ☎282 624 257, ☎282 624 340. Simple, good-value one-bedroom apartments in an ungainly concrete lump that's superbly positioned above the harbour with great sea views. Facilities include a pool. €70.

Pousada do Infante

Sagres ☎282 620 240, ☎www .pousadas.pt. One of the few *pousadas* in the Algarve, this attractive clifftop mansion is decorated with Moorish flourishes. The en-suite rooms are spacious and there are splendid views from the terrace. The clifftop garden boasts a swimming pool and tennis courts, while inside there's a games room, bar and restaurant. €150.

Campsite

Parque de Campismo de Sagres

Cerro das Moitos ☎282 624 351, ☎www.orbitur.pt. Two kilometres northwest of the village, this rather exposed campsite has a pleasing rural setting, though facilities are limited.

Cafés

Café Conchinha

Praça da República 8 ☎282 624 131. Daily 8am–8pm. Very popular tourist spot, thanks to the attractive outside tables on the main square, offering a good range of snacks, including croissants, *tostas* and sandwiches.

Pastelaria Marreiros

Praça da República 12, Sagres ☎282 624 861. Daily 8am–8pm. The clientele is more Portuguese than that of the *Conchinha* next door,

PLACES Sagres and around

▼LIGHTHOUSE AT CABO DE SÃO VICENTE

though the range of snacks and drinks is similar.

Nortada

Praia da Martinhal ☎282 624 147. Daily: May–Oct 10am–midnight; Sept–April Mon & Wed–Thurs 11am–5pm. Jazzy beach bar and café set in a modern wood hut with a terrace right on the sands. Serves a good range of mid-priced international dishes along with the usual Portuguese fare and baguettes; it also does fine milkshakes and fresh juices, and is the base for the local water-sports school.

Restaurants

Bossa Nova

Rua Comandante Matoso 8650, Sagres ☎282 624 566. Tues–Sun noon–11pm. Quietly trendy place noted for its eclectic mix of dishes; choose from the excellent and good-value pizzas, pasta, salads and imaginative vegetarian meals. There are a few tables in the inner courtyard.

Casa Sagres

Praça da República, Sagres. Daily noon–3pm & 6.30–9.30pm. On the road towards Praia da Mareta, this moderately priced restaurant has a superbly positioned terrace overlooking the sea. Pricey but well-cooked specialities include *cataplana* and *arroz de marisco*, while grills are well priced. Around €15–20 for a full meal.

A Grelha

Rua Comandante Matoso, Sagres. Daily noon–3pm & 6–10pm. Simple, family-run grill house with a more local feel than many of the restaurants along this stretch. Meat and fish are good value. Under €15 for a full meal.

Mar á Vista

Sítio da Mareta, Sagres ☎282 624 247. Mon, Tues & Thurs–Sun 10am–midnight. On a scrubby patch of ground just off the road to Praia da Mareta, this pleasant eatery serves a long list of good-value fish, omelettes and salads (around €15 for a full meal), with fine views from its outdoor tables.

Raposo

Praia da Mareta ☎282 624 168. Daily 10am–10pm. Lovely beach bar-restaurant right on the sands, filled with surfers during the day. Most of the meat dishes are good-value although the seafood is expensive.

A Tasca

Porto da Baleeira, Sagres ☎282 624 177. May–Sept daily 8am–midnight; Oct–April closed Wed. Very popular with tour groups and becoming expensive, this is nevertheless the best of Sagres' fish restaurants, with a few meat dishes and superb fish straight from the harbour. Tables outside face the Atlantic, though it's just as fun in the barn-like interior, its walls encrusted with pebbles and old bottles. Expect to pay upwards of €20.

Telheiro

Praia da Mareta ☎282 624 174. Mon & Wed–Sun 9am–11pm. Set on a raised bluff with a superb terrace facing the beach, this is a lovely place for a splurge, with top-quality if pricey fish and seafood such as *arroz de lagosta* (lobster rice) and *cataplana de tamboril e marisco* (seafood and monkfish stew).

Vila Velha

Rua Patrão A. Faustino, Sagres ☎282 624 788. May–Sept daily 6.30–10pm; Oct–April Tues–Sun 6.30–10pm.

In a pretty white house, this upmarket and somewhat formal restaurant serves superior dishes that blend new and traditional Portuguese cuisine, including *tagliatelle com camarão e tamboril* (pasta with shrimp and monkfish). There is usually a vegetarian option and children's menu. Booking is advised. Around €20–25 for a full meal.

Bars

Batedor

Rua das Naus Baleeira, Sagres ☎282 624 810. Daily 8am–2am. Closed Mon Sept–May. A modern café-bar in a superb spot right above the harbour, with an extensive list of drinks – try the lethal caipirinhas – as well as ice creams, snacks and pizzas.

Bubble Lounge

Rua Nossa Senhora da Graça, Sagres ☎282 624 497. May–Sept daily 4pm–3am; Oct–April Tues–Sun 8pm–2am. This groovy surfers' bar has comfy chairs, a screen showing surf movies and ambient sounds.

Dromedário

Rua Comandante Matoso, Sagres ☎282 624 219. Daily 10am–2am. Great little bar with Egyptian-inspired decor, attracting a young clientele. It serves a mean range of cocktails and juices, along with inexpensive pizzas and great breakfasts.

Last Chance Saloon

Sítio da Mareta, Sagres ☎282 624 113. Tues–Sun 6pm–midnight. In a wooden shack overlooking the beach, this is a laid-back place to down an early evening beer or two, and also has Internet access.

Rosa dos Ventos

Praça da República, Sagres ☎282 624 480. Mon & Wed–Sun noon–midnight. Atmospheric bar in an old town house on the main square, which also does simple food. Gets packed most evenings with a young, drunken crowd.

PLACES Sagres and around

The west coast

The Algarve's west coast faces the full brunt of the Atlantic, whose crashing breakers and cooler waters have deterred developers. This is popular territory for surfers, hardy nudists and campervanners, but be warned that the sea can be dangerous and swimmers should take great care. The rocky coastline is punctuated by fantastic broad beaches accessible from the small village Carrapateira, or the prettier and livelier Aljezur and Odeceixe. The designation in 1995 of this entire stretch of coast as a nature reserve – the Parque Natural Sudoeste Alentejano e Costa Vincentina – has restricted development, but that means there is a paucity of accommodation. Public transport serves the main centres, but most of these are set back from the beaches, so your own transport is a distinct advantage.

Map: Atlantic Ocean / Parque Natural da Costa Vicentina showing Praia de Odeceixe, Odeceixe, Maria Vinagre, Rogil, Praia Amoreira, Praia de Monte Clérigo, Vale da Telha, Aljezur, Igreja Nova, Praia da Arrifana, Barranco da Vaca, Praia de Vale de Figueiras, Serra de Espinhaço de Cão, Praia da Bordeira, Carrapateira, Praia do Amado — 0 5 km

Carrapateira and its beaches

Connected by occasional weekday bus from Vila do Bispo. Set in gently rolling countryside studded with aromatic pine and eucalyptus, Carrapateira is a fairly nonde-script village that's little more than a cluster of houses round a hilltop church. However, it is just 3km from **Praia da Bordeira**, one of the best beaches in the entire Algarve.

▼PRAIA DO AMADO

▲ ALJEZUR OLD TOWN

In contrast to the craggy, cliff-backed beaches further south, this spectacular deep stretch of sands spills inland to merge with dunes and the wide river valley behind. The road west from Carrapateira passes a small car park next to the river, from where you cross a narrow stretch of the water onto the back of the beach. Alternatively, carry on up the hill where another car park sits just above the sands. It's a beautiful spot, popular with families; the sandbanks also provide shelter from the wind for an unofficial campsite, which seems to be tolerated by the local police.

Four kilometres south of Praia da Bordeira, along the coast road, lies **Praia do Amado**, which is also signed off the main road just south of Carrapateira. Another fantastic, broad sandy bay backed by low hills with a couple of seasonal cafés, this one is particularly popular with surfers. There's a surf school here (☎ & ℻282 624 560; daily 10.30am–dusk, weather permitting) which offers equipment hire and surf courses from €35.

Aljezur

The village of Aljezur is both the prettiest and liveliest town along the west coast of the Algarve. It is divided into three distinct parts. The main coast road passes through a prosaic, modern lower town with banks, the post office and a range of cafés and restaurants. Another part of Aljezur, Igreja Nova, lies uphill towards Monchique. A pleasant if functional suburb, it takes its name from the "new church" that was built here after the 1755 earthquake in the belief that the residents would move away from the original settlement, though in fact most people preferred to stay put.

The most interesting part of town is the historic old town, which spreads uphill beyond the bridge over the Aljezur river, a network of narrow cobbled streets reaching up between whitewashed houses to the remains of a tenth-century Moorish **castle**. It's a lovely walk to the castle, with sweeping views over the valley, via a motley selection of museums. The first of these, the **Museu**

PLACES   **The west coast**

Visiting Aljezur

There are four buses daily to Aljezur from Lagos via Bensafrim, continuing to Ode-ceixe. A further three buses run daily from Lagos via Portimão to Aljezur, continuing on to Lisbon. The turismo (May–Sept Mon & Fri–Sun 10am–1.30pm & 2.30–5.30pm, Tues–Thurs 9.30am–7pm; Oct–April Mon–Fri 9.30am–1pm & 2.30–6pm; ☎282 998 229) is in Largo do Mercado, by the river and in front of the town market.

Municipal (Largo 5 de Outubro ☎282 991 011; Mon–Fri 10am–12.30pm & 2–5.30pm; €1), is set in the attractive former town hall, housing an eclectic collection of historical artefacts gathered from the region: dusty farm implements, old axes and the like. Note that at quiet times, you have to ask at the Museu Municipal for access to the town's other museums. The best of these is the **Casa Museu Pintor José Cercas** (Rua do Castelo ☎282 991 011; Mon–Fri 10am–12.30pm & 2–5.30pm; €1), which displays the works and collections of local artist José Cercas, who lived in the house until his death in 1992. His well-observed landscapes and religious scenes are complemented by an attractive house with a pretty garden.

Arrifana

Served by two daily buses from Aljezur (May–Sept only). One kilometre south of Aljezur, a road heads down to the longest beach in this stretch at Arrifana, 10km to the southeast. The beach is a fine sandy sweep set below high, crumbling black cliffs. A narrow road leads down to the beach, but in high season all car parking spots are usually taken, which means parking at the top of the cliff, a steep five-minute walk away. The beach is popular with surfers, and surf competitions are sometimes held here. The clifftop boasts the remains of a ruined fort, just up from a cluster of cafés and holiday villas.

Monte Clérigo

Served by two daily buses from Aljezur (May–Sept only). Monte Clérigo is a pretty little holiday village of pink- and white-faced beach houses. A cluster of café-restaurants face a superb, family-oriented beach tucked into the foot of a river valley.

▼PRAIA DA ARRIFANA

Praia Amoreira

The quiet beach of Praia Amoreira (no public transport connections) is accessible off the main Aljezur–Odeceixe road some 5km northwest of Aljezur; the drive here down a broad river valley is delightful. It's another fine sandy bay stretching north of the mouth of the Riba de Aljezur, backed by a handy seasonal beach café.

Odeceixe

Served by 2–3 daily buses from Lagos. The attractive town of Odeceixe tumbles down a hillside opposite the broad valley of the Odeceixe river below the winding, tree-lined main coast road. Sleepy out of season, its character changes in summer when it attracts a steady stream of surfers, camp-ervanners and families, lured by the local beach (see below). Most of the action is centred round the main square, Largo 1° de Maio, from where the beach is signed to the west. Round here you'll find the post office, banks, supermarkets and plenty of places letting out rooms.

Aside from the square, the town's sights are limited to a small covered market and the Adega-Muscu de Odeceixe (Wed–Sun 7pm–11pm; free), an old wine cellar that has been preserved as a museum in its tra-ditional state, full of old barrels and wine-making equipment.

Praia de Odeceixe

Reached down a verdant river valley, the beach – Praia de Odeceixe – lies some 4km to the west of the village. It's a lovely walk following the river to a broad, sandy bay framed by low cliffs. It is one of the most sheltered beaches on this stretch of coast, offering superb surfing and relatively safe swimming,

▲MONTE CLÉRIGO

especially at low tide, or you can splash about in the river itself. A pretty cluster of traditional houses and cafés lie banked up to the south of the bay, though as most are holiday homes it's closed up and largely deserted out of season.

Accommodation

Residencial Dom Sancho

Largo Igreja Nova 1, Igreja Nova, Aljezur ☎ 282 998 119, ✉ turimol@mail .telepac.pt. This modern guest house sits just above the main church overlooking a pedestri-anized street. Rooms are large and comfortable, with bath and TV. €45.

PLACES The west coast

Restaurante Café Dorita

Praia de Odeceixe ☎282 947 581. Closed Nov–April. Simple rooms, the best with sweeping views over the waves, are let out by the restaurant (see opposite) above the beach. One even has a terrace. Those with private bath are €7 extra. Book ahead in high season. €38.

Pensão das Dunas,

Rua da Padaria 9, Carrapateira ☎ & ⊕282 973 118. A very pretty building on the beach-side of the village, this has a number of simple rooms overlooking a flower-filled courtyard; there are apartments for two or four people. The price includes a substantial breakfast. Rooms €25, apartments €37–55.

Hospedaria Firmino Bernardinho

Rua da Praia, Odeceixe ☎282 947 362. At the foot of town on the road out to the beach, this is the most attractive place in town. Spotless, modern rooms with small balconies and bathrooms overlook the wide river valley. €50.

Oceano

Arrifana ☎282 997 300. Restaurant closed Tues. Friendly, all-purpose café, restaurant and guesthouse on the clifftop above the beach. Pleasant rooms come with shower and fine views, while the upstairs restaurant does fine mid-priced fish and grills. €30.

Residêncio do Parque

Rua da Estrada Nacional 11, Odeceixe ☎282 947 117. Run by an eccentric, welcoming owner, this huge house has a mixed bag of rooms – the best on the top floor with small balconies overlooking the valley; all are en suite with TVs. €62.

Campsites

Parque de Campismo Municipal de Aljezur

Vale da Telha ☎282 998 444, ✉vale .telha@clix.pt. Despite its name, this well-equipped campsite is closer to Monte Clérigo beach than Aljezur, at the edge of the sprawling Vale da Telha complex. Nicely sited under trees though you'll need your own transport.

Parque de Campismo do Serrão

Herdade do Serrão, Aljezur ☎282 990 220, ✉camping-serrao@clix.pt. This large, tranquil campsite is set amongst dense trees some 7km northwest of Aljezur. It has its own pool, supermarket and tennis courts.

Cafés

Pastelaria Mioto

Rua 25 de Abril, Loja H, Aljezur ☎282 998 803. Daily 6am–midnight. A neat, modern *pastelaria* tucked into the back of a shopping centre. It offers a fine range of cakes and pastries, but the main appeal is a superb terrace overlooking the verdant river valley behind.

Paraíso do Mar

Praia Amoreira ☎282 997 239. May–Sept daily 10am–7pm. A superbly positioned café-restaurant facing the beach: the perfect place for an early evening beer. It also does snacks and moderately priced grilled meat and fish.

Café Praia do Armado

Praia do Armado. April–Sept daily 10am–8pm. A lively beach café, where the surfers retreat for drinks and inexpensive snacks.

Restaurants

Blue Sky

Largo 1 de Maio, Odeceixe. Daily
8am–midnight. Popular travellers'
spot on the main square offering
inexpensive *petiscos*, pizzas, pasta
and drinks. A good place to
catch the last rays of the day.

Restaurante Café Dorita

Praia de Odeceixe ☏282 947 581.
Tues–Sun 10am–10pm, closed
Nov–April. On the road above the
beach, this simple café-restaurant
offers mid-priced Portuguese
food best enjoyed on the outside
terrace overlooking the beach. It
also lets out rooms (see opposite).

Pont a Pé

Largo da Liberdade 16, Aljezur ☏282
998 104. Mon–Sat 12.30–3pm &
7–11pm. Moderately priced grills
are served at this cosy diner up
by the tourist office, though
even more appealing is the riverside terrace complete with
table football. Live music most
weekends competes with the
sound of the resident frogs.

O Retiro do Adelino

Rua Nova 20, Odeceixe. Daily noon–
3pm & 6–11pm. Bumper portions
of inexpensive grilled chicken,
fish with tomato rice and *feijoada*
are served at this friendly grill
house with a little courtyard.

Restaurante Ruth

Rua 25 de Abril 14, Aljezur ☏282
998 534. Mon–Fri & Sun noon–3pm
& 6–11pm. This highly regarded
restaurant specializes in moderately priced regional dishes,
including the local speciality,
sweet potatoes. Along with daily
specials it has superb *arroz de
tamboril com camarão* (monkfish
and prawn rice).

O Sitio do Rio

Praia do Bordeira. Mon & Wed–Sun
noon–10pm. Closed Nov. Around
1km back from Praia do Bordeira towards Carrapateira,
this restaurant offers superb,
mid-priced organic and free-
range Portuguese food, with an
outdoor terrace.

O Zé

Monte Clérigo ☏282 998 621.
Tues–Sun 9am–10pm. The best
positioned of Monte Clérigo's
café-restaurants, with decently
priced snacks, drinks and full
Portuguese meals. The tables out
the back face the beach.

Essentials

Arrival

Year-round schedule and charter flights serve Faro's modern **international airport**, 6km west of the town centre. The airport has various standard facilities – a bank with an ATM machine, shops, post office and a tourist office (daily 8am–11.30pm; ☎ 289 818 582). A number of car rental companies also have offices at the airport. Most use a special car park right opposite the terminal, though some use a less convenient dropping-off point five minutes away; check with the company when you collect your car (see Directory for details).

To get public transport to other towns in the Algarve means a short journey to Faro's central bus or train stations. Buses #14 and #16 run from the airport via both stations, which are a few minutes away from each other. The 20–25-minute ride costs €1.20 (7.10am–9pm, 8pm at weekends, roughly every 45min). To reach Faro by taxi from the airport is a ten- to fifteen-minute ride, which should cost about €10; there's also a twenty percent surcharge between 10pm and 6am and at weekends. For details of train and bus travel, see below.

Transport

Trains are the least expensive form of public transport, if on the slow side. The Algarve rail line runs from Lagos to Vila Real de Santo António on the Spanish border, linking with the Lisbon line (for connections to the continent) at Tunes. Going from west to east, you may have to change at Tunes, Faro or Tavira, depending on your destination. Free train timetables for the Algarve line are available from information desks at main stations, or ☎ 808 208 208. For national routes and fares, check ⓦ www.cp.pt. Always turn up at the station with time to spare, as long queues often form at the ticket desk, though some smaller regional stations are sometimes unmanned, in which case just hop on and pay the ticket inspector on board. Children under four go free; under-12s pay half price. Senior citizens (over-65s) can get thirty percent off travel if they produce their passport (or other form of ID proving their age) and ask for a *Bihete terceira Idade*. Lastly, note that some train stations are quite far from the town or village they serve and there's no guarantee of connecting transport.

It's almost always quicker to go by **bus** than by rail, if you can, though you'll pay slightly more. The main regional bus company is EVA (routes and timetables on ⓦ www.eva-transportes.pt). Comfortable express buses operate on longer routes, including to Seville and Spain, for which you'll usually have to reserve tickets in advance. For other destinations in Portugal, the main carrier is Rede Expressos (fares and routes on ⓦ www.rede-expressos.pt).

Local bus stations (detailed in the text) are the place to pick up timetables and reserve seats. Note that services are considerably less frequent and occasionally non-existent at weekends.

Car rental and taxis

Car rental rates are among the lowest in Europe, but petrol (*gasolina*) is relatively expensive. Most rental cars run on unleaded (*sem chumbo*), and some on diesel (*gasoil*). Driving licences from EU countries are accepted, otherwise an international driving licence is required. In large towns there are usually car parks where you pay by the hour, along with pay-and-display parking bays, for which you'll need exact change, although spaces are often at a premium in high season. You're also likely to see the unemployed pointing you to empty spaces; it's best to tip (around €0.50) for this service.

Traffic drives on the right: speed limits are 50kph in towns and villages; 90kph on normal roads; and 120kph on the motorways. At road junctions, unless there's a sign to the contrary, vehicles coming from the right have priority. If you're stopped by the police, they'll want to see your documents – carry them in the car at all times. Don't leave anything of value in an unattended car. See p.192 for car hire companies.

Travelling by **taxi** in Portugal is relatively cheap and is worth considering for trips across major towns and for shorter journeys in rural areas. Generally, taxis are metered, with a minimum fare of €1.60. Additional charges are made for carrying baggage in the boot and for travelling between 10pm and 6am and at weekends. Outside major towns, you can negotiate if you want to hire a taxi for a few hours.

Bikes and mopeds

Bicycles are a great way of seeing the region, though pedalling can be hard work as everywhere much inland from the coast and away from the Rio Guadiana is hilly. Several special shops, hotels, campsites and youth hostels rent out bikes for around €5–10 a day. You can also rent mopeds, scooters and low-powered (80cc) **motorbikes** in many of the resorts, with hire costs starting at around €25 a day. You need to be at least 18 to hire these (and over 23 to rent larger bikes over 125cc) and to have held a full licence for at least a year. Rental usually includes helmet hire and locks along with third-party insurance.

Money

Despite being the most expensive region in Portugal, the Algarve remains notably cheaper than northern Europe and North America. Portugal is one of the twelve European Union countries to use the euro. Euro notes are issued in denominations of 5, 10, 20, 50, 100, 200 and 500 euro, and coins in denominations of 1, 2, 5, 10, 20 and 50 cents and 1 and 2 euro.

You'll find a **bank** in all but the smallest towns, and many have automatic exchange facilities. Standard opening hours are Monday to Friday 8.30am to 3pm. Changing cash in banks is easy and shouldn't attract more than €3 commission.

By far the easiest way to get money in Portugal is to use **ATMs** (called *Multibanco*). You'll find them in even the most out-of-the-way small towns, and you can withdraw up to €200 per day. Check with your bank to see whether you can use your credit or debit card in the Algarve, and remember that on credit card withdrawals you'll be charged interest from day one in addition to the usual currency conversion fee. Most Portuguese banks will give cash advances on cards over the counter, charging a currency conversion fee. Credit cards are also accepted in many hotels and restaurants.

Banks in Portugal charge an outrageous commission for changing **travellers' cheques** (upwards of €13 per transaction). However, more reasonable fees can be had in *caixas* – savings banks or building societies – and some exchange bureaux that often open in the evening. Larger hotels are sometimes willing to change travellers' cheques at low commission (though often at poor conversion rates). It's worth taking a supply in case your plastic is lost, stolen or swallowed by an ATM.

Accommodation

Most accommodation in the Algarve is fairly modern and there is a wide range to choose from. If you're travelling in high season (June to early Sept) you should try to reserve in advance

Rooms and guest-houses

Some of the cheapest accommodation consists of **rooms** (*quartos* or *dormidas*) let out in private houses. These are sometimes advertised, or more often hawked at bus and train stations, and they can be good value. The local turismo may also have a list of rooms available. It's always worth haggling, and check the room is not too far from the centre. If you're not paying in advance, get the owner to write down the agreed price for you.

The main budget travel standby is a room in a **pensão** – officially graded from one to three stars (often, it seems, in a quite random fashion). Better ones usually have TVs and en-suite facilities. Many serve meals, but they rarely insist that you take them. *Pensões* that don't serve meals are sometimes called *residenciais* (singular *residencial* or *residência*). Similar to *pensões*, and generally at the cheaper end of the scale, are *hospedarias* or *casas de hóspedes* – boarding houses – which can be characterful places.

Hotels, inns and pousadas

A one-star **hotel** usually costs about the same as a three-star *pensão*, and is often similar in standard. Prices for two- and three-star hotels, though, see a notable shift upwards, with facilities such as a bar, restaurant or pool.

Rates for the four- and five-star hotel league are closer to those in northern Europe, with facilities to match, such as gyms, babysitting services and children's clubs. Similar to four- and five-star hotels are inns, called *estalagens* or *albergarias*.

Pousadas (literally "resting places") are part-government owned hotels, usually in historic buildings or castles. The Algarve has two characterful if slightly formal *pousadas*, but there are plans to open more; details are in the text (p.74 and p.173), or visit ⓦ www.pousadas.pt.

Villas, apartments and youth hostels

Virtually every area of the Algarve has some sort of **villa** or **apartment** available for hire, from simple one-room apartments to luxurious five- or six-bed houses complete with gardens and swimming pools. High summer sees the best places booked up months in advance (holiday and tour operators are useful if you want to book ahead). Expect to pay at least €70 a night in high season for an apartment for two people, up to €140 for a top villa. Outside peak period you should be able to turn up and bag somewhere for around 25 percent less, and 50 percent less in winter.

There are five **youth hostels** (*pousadas de juventude*) in the Algarve, most open all year round. Details are in the text, or see ⓦ www.pousadasjuventude.pt.

Campsites

The Algarve has a number of authorized **campsites**, many in very attractive locations and, despite their often large size (over 500 spaces is not uncommon), extremely crowded in summer. Most of the campsites have spaces for campervans and caravans and many also have permanent caravans and bungalows for hire. Charges are per person and per caravan or tent, with showers and parking extra; even so, it's rare that you'll end up paying more than €5 a person, although those operated by the Orbitur chain (ⓦ www.orbitur.pt) are usually a little more expensive. Sites are detailed in the text, or see @ www.roteiro-campista.pt.

Camping outside official grounds is not allowed in the Algarve, though you'll rarely have problems parking a campervan behind some of the best, out-of-the-way beaches. Be warned, too, that thefts from campsites are a regular occurrence.

Information

You can pick up free brochures and maps from the Portuguese tourist office in your home country. Once in Portugal, get hold of a copy of the excellent *Turismo do Algarve Guide*, a monthly listings magazine in English and Portuguese, available free from most tourist offices and hotels.

You'll find a **turismo** (tourist office) in almost every town and village. Details are given in the text; the offices are usually helpful and friendly, and English is spoken, though note that opening times tend to be fluid, depending on the availability of staff. There's also an excellent freephone line, Linha Verde Turista ☎800 296 296 (Mon–Sat 9am–midnight, Sun & holidays 9am–8pm); the operators speak English and have information on museums, transport, accommodation, restaurants, hospitals, and police stations.

The Portuguese National Tourist Office and turismos can provide you with a reasonable map of the country (1:600,000), which is fine for everything except mountain roads. If you're doing any real exploration, however, it's worth investing in a good road map. The best available is the *Rough Guide Map: The Algarve* (1:100,000).

Most resorts sell international **newspapers** – often the previous day's. *The News* (@ www.the-news.net) is an English-language weekly national, while the *Algarve Resident* is a weekly covering local news and events.

Useful websites

@ **www.algarvenet.com** Detailed site dedicated to the Algarve, covering everything from tourist sites to weather and shopping.

@ **www.maisturismo.pt** Search engine for hotels, mostly business-orientated or at the top end of the market.

@ **www.min-cultura.pt/Agenda/Agenda .html** The Ministry of Culture's website, with details of events in major Algarve towns.

@ **www.portugal.org** Government-run tourist site, with an Algarve section.

@ **www.Portugal-info.net** Links to various sites covering everything from accommodation and flights to the weather.

@ **www.portugalvirtual.pt** Links with extensive hotel and villa listings, restaurants and bars, as well as sports information.

@ **www.rtalgarve.pt** The official tourist board site. Information is useful if limited and not always regularly updated.

Food and drink

Portuguese food tends to be inexpensive and served in big portions, and even the humblest bar can serve one of Portugal's excellent local wines. At their finest, dishes can be superb, made with fresh ingredients bursting with flavour. Grilled meats and fish tend to be the best bets, usually accompanied by chips, rice or boiled potatoes and salad. But don't expect sophisticated sauces or delicate touches: stews, in particular, are not for the faint-hearted; offal features highly on many menus and even the ever-present *bacalhau* (salted dried cod) can be heavy going if you choose the wrong variety.

Though there are plenty of international **restaurants** round the Algarve, Portuguese restaurants tend to be of high quality and very good value. It's always worth checking the *ementa turística* – a set three-course meal, including a drink – and the *prato do dia* (dish of the day), which often features a local speciality. As well as restaurants, you can find *tascas* (small taverns), a *casa de pasto* (inexpensive diner, often lunches only) and a *churrascaria* (specializing in grilled meat and fish). A *cervejaria* is literally a "beer house", more informal than a restaurant and offering drinks and snacks as well as full meals. Finally, a *marisqueira* has a superior fish- and seafood-based menu. Most restaurants are open noon–3pm for lunch and 7.30–11pm for dinner. All places have a cover charge for bread, but remember that any other starters put on your table will be charged for – tell the waiter if you do not want them.

In this guide, we have rated a two-course meal with a drink as inexpensive for under €10, mid-priced at €10–20, and expensive at over €20.

There is little to distinguish many **cafés and bars** in Portugal, and most sell both coffee and alcohol throughout the day. *Pastelarias* specialize in pastries and cakes (*bolos*) and are also good stops for breakfast croissants and breads. For light lunches, cafés and bars do snacks that usually include *rissóis de carne* (meat patties), *pastéis de bacalhau/carne/camerão* (salted cod/meat/shrimp rissoles), *chouriço* (smoked sausage) and *sandes de queijo/fiambre* (cheese or ham sandwiches). Coffee is invariably fresh and of good quality. *Uma bica* is a strong espresso, *um galão* is a weak milky coffee in a tall glass, while *uma café com leite* is a normal coffee with milk. Children are welcome in most bars, where you can buy soft drinks as well as inexpensive local drinks such as Sagres or Super Bock beer and gigantic measures of spirits. Local firewaters include *medronho*, made from the fruit of the strawberry tree, *Algarviana*, made from almonds, and *brandymel*, a honey brandy.

Festivals and events

February
Carnival Loulé has one of the best of the region's lively carnival parades, with costumed processions through town.

March/April
Aleluia procession, Easter Sunday São Brás de Alportel has the most distinctive of the region's various Easter processions.
Mãe Soberana, Loulé The Algarve's biggest religious festival begins when the image of Our Lady of Piety is carried from the hilltop church of Nossa Senhora da Piedade to the Church of São Francisco on Easter Sunday before being returned two weeks later in a solemn procession.

May 1
Atacar o Maio Literally "attacking May", when May 1 is celebrated with dried figs and *medronho* brandy accompanied by folk music. In Monchique, *medronho* is drunk and *mel* (honey) is eaten with *Bolo do Tacho* – pot cake made from corn flour, honey and chocolate. In Estoi, pine cones and rosemary are laid at the church of Our Lady of Pé da Cruz, with an evening torchlit procession and fireworks.
Alte Week of Arts and Culture Live shows, brass bands and folk dancing are accompanied by a grand picnic in May.
Algarve International Cinema Festival Cinemas in Portimão, Alvor and Praia da Rocha screen films from both Portuguese

and international directors throughout May.

June–August

Algarve International Music Festival
The biggest cultural event in the Algarve, organized by the Gulbenkian Foundation and others, with chamber music, ballet and top international artists performing at venues throughout the region.

Festa de Santo António (June 12–13) A celebration of one of the most important of the popular saints, with music, food, drink and all-night dancing in Faro, Tavira, Quarteira and smaller towns.

Festa de São João (June 23–24) Processions and music throughout the region – especially Lagoa, Lagos, Monchique and Portimão, for São João (Saint John).

Festa de São Pedro (June 28–29) St Peter is the last of the popular saints' days celebrated with revelry until the small hours.

July

Loulé International Jazz Festival Local and international jazz performers play at weekends throughout July.

Feira do Carmo, Faro The town's big annual fair, with handicrafts and live entertainment. Also celebrated with a parade of boats at Fuzeta.

International Motorcycle Concentration Annual leather-clad celebration with rock bands playing between Faro beach and Faro airport.

August

Fatacil, Lagoa Big agricultural trade fair in mid-August with displays of local goods backed by music and entertainment.

Coimbra Serenades Top Coimbra Fado – the distinctly Portuguese version of the blues – is performed throughout the region in August.

Medieval Days, Castro Marim Recreations of medieval jousts and pageants, usually late August.

Espectáculos de Folclore Folk performances around the Algarve in August and September with a grande finale on Portimão's waterfront.

October

Feira de Santa Iria, Largo de São Francisco, Faro Second of the big Faro fairs, with a week of craft stalls, bumper cars, music and daily festivities in October.

Food festivals

January
Smoked Sausage Fair, Querença. Somewhat ironically celebrates Saint Luís, the patron saint of animals.

March
Smoked Sausage Fair, Monchique. Local produce market and special menus in restaurants.

May
Gastronomy Festival, Portimão. Restaurants serve typically Portuguese dishes from various regions.

June
Week of Portuguese Gastronomy, Lagoa. Gourmets prepare the best of Portuguese food, plus a handicrafts fair.

July
Beer Festival, Silves. Held in the Fábrica Inglês, with beers from around the world.
Sweet Fair, Lagos. Sculpted egg, almond and fig sweets are sold along with other local produce.

Presunto Festival, Monchique. The place to try cured hams, in the town famed for them.

August
Festival do Marisco, Olhão. Fish and seafood festival with live music.
Sardine Festival, Quarteira. An enormous grill on the beach cooks several hundred kilos of fish.
Petiscos Festival, Querença. A celebration of small tapas-like dishes accompanied by dancing and music.

September
Sweet potato and barnacle festival, Aljezur. The west coast town shows off its local specialities, accompanied by live entertainment.

November
Chestnut festival, Marmelete, Alferce and Vale Silves. More fresh food and revelry accompanies the autumn harvests.

October–November
Autumn Fairs Stalls sell food and handi-crafts at markets throughout the region in October and November.
São Martinho (November 11) Saint's day celebrated by eating roasted chestnuts – especially round the mountain village of Monchique – and drinking *agua pé* ("foot water"), the first tasting of this year's wine harvest.

December 24
Christmas Eve Christmas Eve is the main Christmas celebration, with a traditional *bacalhau* supper after midnight Mass.

December 31
New Year's Eve Enthusiastic banging of pots and pans heralds the new year, with live entertainment and fireworks throughout the region.

Algarve's golf courses

The following is a round-up of the main courses, listed according to the nearest main town or resort. See pp.28–29 for more on golf and for general websites.

Albufeira (p.107)
Pine Cliffs Praia da Falésia ☎ 289 500 113, ✆ 289 500 117. No handicap certificate required.
Salgados ☎ 289 583 030, ✆ 289 591 112. No handicap certificate required.

Alvor (p.139)
Alto Golf Quinta do Alto do Poço ☎ 282 460 873, ✉ golf@altogolf.com. Handicap max 28 men; 36 women.
Penina Golf Club, Penina ☎ 282 420 223, ✆ 282 420 300. Handicap max 28 men; 36 women.

Carvoeiro (p.124)
Gramacho ☎ 282 340 900, ✆ 282 340 901. No handicap certificate required.
Vale de Milho ☎ 282 358 502, ✆ 282 358 497. No handicap certificate required.
Vale de Pinta ☎ 282 340 900, ✆ 282 340 901. Handicap max 27 men; 35 women.

Castro Marim (p.101)
Castro Marim Golf ☎ 281 510 330, ✆ 281 510 338. No handicap certificate required.

Lagos (p.151)
Boavista ☎ 282 782 151, ✆ 282 782 150. No handicap certificate required.

Manta Rota/Altura (p.93)
Quinta da Ria/Quinta de Cima Vila Nova de Cacela ☎ 281 950 580, ✆ 281 950 589. No handicap certificate required.

Meia Praia (p.155)
Palmares ☎ 282 790 500, ✆ 282 790 509. Handicap max 28 men; 36 women.

Quarteira (p.62)
Vila Sol Morgadinhos Alto de Semino, Quarteira/Vilamoura ☎ 289 316 499, ✆ 289 300 591. Handicap max 24 men; 35 women.

Quinta do Lago (p.61)
São Lorenço ☎ 289 396 522, ✆ 289 396 908. Handicap max 28 men; 36 women.
Quinta do Lago/Ria Formosa ☎ 289 390 700, ✆ 289 394 013. Handicap max 26 men; 35 women.
Pinheiros Altos ☎ 289 359 910, ✆ 289 394 392. Handicap max 28 men; 36 women.

Salema (p.163)
Parque da Floresta Vale do Poço ☎ 282 690 054, ✆ 282 695 157. No handicap certificate required.

Tavira (p.83)
Benamor Quinta de Benamor ☎ 281 320 880, ✆ 281 320 888. Handicap max 28 men; 36 women.

Vale de Lobo (p.62)
Vale Do Lobo ☎ 289 353 535, ✉ golf@etvdla.pt. Handicap max 28 men (Ocean Course), 27 (Royal Course), 36 women (Ocean Course), 35 (Royal Course).

Vilamoura (p.63)
Laguna (Vilamoura III) ☎ 289 310 180, ✆ 289 310 183. Handicap 28 men; 36 women.
Millennium ☎ 289 310 188, ✆ 289 310 183. Handicap max 24 men; 28 women.
The Old Course (Vilamoura I) ☎ 289 310

341, ☎289 310 321. Handicap max 24
men; 28 women.
Pinhal (Vilamoura II) ☎289 310 390,
☎289 310 393. Handicap 28 men; 36
women.

Victoria ☎289 320 100 or 289 310 333,
✉reserves_golfe@lusotour.pt. Handicap 24
men; 28 women.

Directory

Addresses Addresses are written with
the name of the road first followed by the
number. The numbers 1°, 2° etc mean
first, second floor etc. The ground floor
(first floor in US) is marked r/c (*rés-do-
chão*). You may also see d/dto or e/esq
after the number, which mean on the right
(*direito*) or left (*esquerda*) of the main
staircase.

Airlines British Airways (☎808 200 125,
✆www.british-airways.com); Portugália
(Lisbon ☎218 425 559, ✆www.pga.pt
/atrio); TAP Air Portugal, Rua Dom Francisco Gomes 8, Faro (☎289 800 200,
✆www.tap-airportugal.pt).

Airport flight information ☎289 800
800.

Car hire companies AutoJardim (☎800
200 613, ✆www.auto-jardim.com); Avis
(☎800 201 002, ✆www.avis.com.pt);
Hertz (☎800 238 238, ✆www.hertz.com);
LuzCar-Sociedade (also hires motorbikes),
Lagos (☎282 761 016).

Children Most hotels and guesthouses can
provide cots free of charge if given advance
notice, and discounts are usually offered
for children who share their parents' room.
International-brand baby foods and nappies
are widely available from supermarkets
and chemists, though fresh milk (*leite do
dia*) can usually only be bought from larger
supermarkets. Some restaurants offer
children's menus – alternatively, nearly all
do half portions (*meia doce*). Take great
care with the sun – children should be
covered up or in the shade between 11am
and 3pm.

Cinemas Most of the larger towns have
cinemas, often inexpensive multiplexes
showing the latest blockbusters. Films are
shown in original language with Portuguese
subtitles.

Consulates Canada, Rua Frei Lourenço
Santa Maria 1–1°, Apt. 79, Faro (☎289

803 757); Denmark, Rua Conselheiro Bívar
10–1°, Faro (☎289 805 561); Netherlands,
Largo Francisco Sá Carneiro 52, Faro
(☎289 820 903); UK Largo Francisco A.
Maurício 7–1°, Apt. 609, Portimão (☎282
490 750). Most countries also have
embassies in Lisbon.

Disabled access Portuguese people will
go out of their way to make your visit as
straightforward as possible, though special
facilities remain limited. There are adapted
WCs and wheelchair facilities at the airport
and reserved disabled parking spaces in
main cities, where the Orange Badge is
recognized. National tourist offices can
supply a list of wheelchair-accessible hotels
and campsites; some are listed in the text,
or contact Wheeling Around the Algarve
(☎289 393 636, ✆www.player.pt),
who organize holiday accommodation,
transport and sporting/leisure activities. A
useful booklet, *Accessible Tourism Guide
of the Algarve Area*, can be obtained from
✉snripd@snripd.mts.gov.pt.

Electricity Portugal uses two-pin plugs
(220v). UK appliances will work with a
continental adaptor.

Emergencies ☎112 for fire, police and
ambulance.

Football The Algarve is not the traditional hotbed of Portuguese soccer, though
Farense from Faro and Portimonense
from Portimão have had spells in the top
division. Top international games are sometimes held at the Faro-Loulé stadium (see
p.55). The season runs from September to
May. For details of fixtures, see ✆www
.portuguese.soccer.com, or buy the daily
sports paper, *A Bola*.

Gay travellers Though traditionally a con-
servative and macho society, Portugal has
become increasingly tolerant of homosexu-
ality. The Lisbon-based Centro Comunitário
Gay e Lesbica de Lisboa (☎218 873 918,

Wed–Sat 6pm–midnight) publish gay listings on @www.ilga-portugal.org. Reader-vote listings can also be found on @www.portugalgay.pt, though the information – in Portuguese – is not updated regularly.

Hospitals Hospital Distrital de Faro, Leão Penedo, Faro ☎289 891 100; Hospital Distrital, Rua do Castelo dos Governadores, Lagos ☎282 763 034; Hospital do Barlavento Algarvio, Sítio do Poço Seco, Portimão ☎282 450 330. There are also various private clinics; get details from the local tourist office.

Internet and mail Post offices (*correios*) are normally open Mon–Fri 8.30am to 6.30pm. Nearly all post offices contain terminals for Internet access, for which prepaid cards can be bought at the counter. Stamps (*selos*) are sold at post offices, from automatic machines on streets and anywhere that has the sign "Correio de Portugal – Selos" displayed.

Opening times Official opening times are given in the text, but note that for many cafés, shops, restaurants and tourist offices, opening times are not rigidly adhered to. This is especially so in smaller places and out of season, when places may open late or not at all in bad weather or during quiet periods. Typical shopping hours are Monday to Friday, 9am–12.30pm & 2.30–7/8pm and Saturday 9am–1pm. Larger supermarkets and many resort shops open daily, often until 11pm.

Pharmacies Pharmacies are open Mon–Fri 9am–1pm & 3–7pm, Sat 9am–1pm. Local papers carry information about 24hr pharmacies, and the details are posted on every pharmacy door.

Public holidays Official holidays are: January 1 (New Year's Day); February/March (Carnival); Good Friday; April 25 (celebrating the 1974 revolution); May 1 (Labour Day); June 10 (Portugal Day and Camões Day); August 15 (Feast of the Assumption); October 5 (Republic Day); November 1 (All Saints' Day); December 1 (Independence Day, celebrating independence from Spain in 1640); December 8 (Immaculate Conception); December 24–25 (Christmas).

Sunbathing Portugal can be traditional and formal: topless bathing is rare on town beaches, though nudism is common on more out-of-the-way beaches.

Time Portugal is on the same time zone as the UK: GMT (late Oct to late March) and BST (late March to late Oct). This is five hours ahead of Eastern Standard Time and eight hours ahead of Pacific Standard Time.

Tipping Service charges are normally included in hotel bills and in the larger restaurants. Smaller restaurants, cafés and bars do not expect a large tip; simply round up the change or leave ten percent of the bill.

Toilets There are very few public toilets. However, nearly all the main tourist sights have a public toilet (*casa de banho*, *retrete*, *hanheiro*, *lavabos* or *WC*), and it is not difficult to sneak into a café or restaurant. Gents are usually marked H (*homens*) or C (*cabalheiros*), and ladies M (*mulheres*) or S (*senhoras*).

Women will experience few problems travelling alone in the Algarve: they may attract some unwanted attention in the beach resorts, but it is unlikely to be insistent or threatening.

Language

Language

English is widely spoken throughout the Algarve, but you will find a few words of Portuguese extremely useful if you are travelling on public transport or in more out-of-the-way places. If you have some knowledge of Spanish, you won't have much problem reading Portuguese. Understanding it when it's spoken, though, is a different matter: pronunciation is entirely different and at first even the easiest words are hard to distinguish. Once you've started to figure out the words it gets a lot easier very quickly.

A useful word is *há* (the H is silent), which means "there is" or "is there?" and can be used for just about anything. Thus: *"Há uma pensão aqui?"* ("Is there a pension here?"). More polite and better in shops or restaurants are *"Tem...?"* (pronounced *taying*) which means "Do you have...?", or *"Queria..."* ("I'd like..."). And of course there are the old standards "Do you speak English?" (*Fala Inglês?*) and "I don't understand" (*Não compreendo*).

Pronunciation

The chief difficulty with pronunciation is its lack of clarity – consonants tend to be slurred, vowels nasal and often ignored altogether. The **consonants** are, at least, consistent:

C is soft before E and I, hard otherwise unless it has a cedilla – *açucar* (sugar) is pronounced "assookar".

CH is somewhat softer than in English; *chá* (tea) sounds like Shah.

J is pronounced like the "s" in pleasure, as is G except when it comes before a "hard" vowel (A, O and U).

LH sounds like "lyuh" (Alcantarilha).

Q is always pronounced as a "k".

S before a consonant or at the end of a word becomes "sh," otherwise it's as in English – Sagres is pronounced "Sahgresh".

X is also pronounced "sh"– *caixa* (cash desk) is pronounced "kaisha".

Vowels are worse – flat and truncated, they're often difficult for English-speaking tongues to get around. The only way to learn is to listen: accents, Ã, Õ, or É, turn them into longer, more familiar sounds.

When two vowels come together they continue to be enunciated separately except in the case of **El** and **OU** – which sound like "a" and long "o" respectively. E at the end of a word is silent unless it has an accent, so that *carne* (meat) is pronounced "karn", while *café* sounds much as you'd expect. The **tilde over Ã or Õ** renders the pronunciation much like the French -an and -on endings only more nasal. More common is **ÃO** (as in *pão*, bread – *são*, saint – *limão*, lemon), which sounds something like a strangled yelp of "Ow!" cut off in midstream.

Words and phrases

Basics

yes; no	sim; não
hello; good morning	olá; bom dia
good afternoon/ night	boa tarde/noite
goodbye, see you later	adeus, até logo
today; tomorrow	hoje; amanhã
please	por favor/ se faz favor
everything all right?	tudo bem?
it's all right/OK	está bem
thank you	obrigado/a*
where; what	onde; que
when; why	quando; porquê
how; how much	como; quanto
I don't know	não sei
do you know . . .?	sabe . . .?
could you . . .?	pode . . .?
sorry; excuse me	desculpe; com licença
this; that	este/a; esse/a
now; later	agora; mais tarde
more; less	mais; menos
big; little	grande; pequeno
open; closed	aberto; fechado
women; men	senhoras; homens
toilet/bathroom	lavabo/quarto de banho
tourist office	turismo
beach	praia
church	igreja
garden	jardim
market	mercado
museum	museu
park	parque
square	praça/largo
cathedral	sé

Obrigado agrees with the sex of the person speaking – a woman says *obrigada*, a man *obrigado*.

Getting around

left, right, straight ahead	esquerda, direita, sempre em frente
here; there	aqui; ali
near; far	perto; longe
Where is the	Onde é a estação
bus station?	de camionetas?
the bus stop for ..	a paragem de autocarro para...
Where does the bus to . . . leave from?	Donde parte o autocarro para...?
What time does it leave?	A que horas parte?
(arrive at . . .?)	(chega a . . .?)
Stop here please	Pare aqui por favor
ticket (to)	bilhete (para)
round trip	ida e volta

Accommodation

I'd like a room	Queria um quarto
It's for one night (week)	É para uma noite (semana)
It's for one person two people	É para uma pessoa (duas pessoas)
How much is it?	Quanto custa?
May I see/ look around?	Posso ver?
Is there a cheaper room?	Há um quarto mais barato?
with a shower	com duche
Inn	pousada
Youth hostel	pousada de juventude

Shopping

How much is it?	Quanto é?
bank; change	banco; câmbio
post office	correios
(two) stamps	(dois) selos
What's this called in Portuguese?	Como se diz isto em Português?
What's that?	O que é isso?
craft shop	artesanato
chemist	farmácia

Days of the week

Sunday	domingo
Monday	segunda-feira
Tuesday	terça-feira
Wednesday	quarta-feira
Thursday	quinta-feira
Friday	sexta-feira
Saturday	sábado

Common Portuguese signs

Aberto	open	Obras	road or building works
Desvio	diversion (on road)	Perigo/Perigoso	danger/dangerous
Dormidas	private rooms for rent	Paragem	bus stop
Elevador	lift	Pré-pagamento	pay in advance
Entrada	entrance	Proibido estacionar	no parking
Fecha a porta	close the door		
Fechado	closed	Saída	exit

Numbers

1	um	17	dezassete
2	dois	18	dezoito
3	três	19	dezanove
4	quatro	20	vinte
5	cinco	21	vinte e um
6	seis	30	trinta
7	sete	40	quarenta
8	oito	50	cinquenta
9	nove	60	sessenta
10	dez	70	setenta
11	onze	80	oitenta
12	doze	90	noventa
13	treze	100	cem
14	catorze	101	cento e um
15	quinze	200	duzentos
16	dezasseis	500	quinhentos
		1000	mil

Food and drink

Places to eat and drink

adega	literally a wine cellar; also does food
casa de pasto	a lunchtime diner
cervejaria	a beer hall, also does food
churrasqueria	a grill house
marisqueira	restaurant specializing in fish and seafood
pastelaria	a patisserie
taberna	a tavern

Basic words and terms

almoço	lunch
assado	roasted
colher	spoon
conta	bill
copo	glass
cozido	boiled
ementa	menu
estrelado/frito	fried
faca	knife
fumado	smoked
garfo	fork
garrafa	bottle
grelhado	grilled
jantar	dinner
mexido	scrambled
pastéis de nata	flaky custard tartlets
pequeno almoço	breakfast
petiscos	tapas-like snacks

Soups, salad and staples

arroz	rice
azeitonas	olives
batatas fritas	chips/french fries
caldo verde	cabbage soup
fruta	fruit

LANGUAGE

Menu glossary

gaspacho	chilled vegetable soup
legumes	vegetables
manteiga	butter
ovos	eggs
pão	bread
pimenta	pepper
piri-piri	chilli sauce
queijo	cheese
sal	salt
salada	salad
sopa de legumes	vegetable soup
sopa de marisco	shellfish soup
sopa de peixe	fish soup

Fish and shellfish

arroz de marisco	seafood rice
atum	tuna
bacalhau à brás	salted cod with egg and potatoes
caldeirada	fish stew
camarões	shrimp
carapau	mackerel
cataplana	fish, shellfish or meat stewed in a circular metal dish
cherne	stone bass
dourada	bream
espada	scabbard fish
espadarte	swordfish
feijoada	rich bean stew, with fish or meat
gambas	prawns
lagosta	lobster
lampreia	lamprey
lulas (grelhadas)	squid (grilled)
pescada	hake
polvo	octopus
mexilhões	mussels
robalo	sea bass
salmonete	red mullet
salmão	salmon
sapateira	crab
santola	spider crab
sardinhas na brasa	charcoal-grilled sardines

truta	trout
viera	scallop

Meat

bife à portuguesa	thin beef steak with a fried egg on top
borrego	lamb
chouriço	spicy sausage
coelho	rabbit
cozido à portuguesa	boiled casserole of meats and beans, served with rice and vegetables
dobrada	tripe
espetada mista	mixed meat kebab
fiambre	ham
febras	pork steaks
frango no churrasco	barbecued chicken
pato	duck
perdiz	partridge
perú	turkey
carne de porco à alentejana	pork cooked with clams
presunto	smoked ham
vitela	veal

Drinks

um copo/ uma garrafa de/da...	a glass/bottle of...
vinho branco/tinto	white/red wine
cerveja	beer
água (sem/com gás)	water (with/without gas)
sumo de laranja/ maçã	orange/apple juice
chá/café	tea/coffee
sem/com leite	without/with milk
sem/com açúcar	without/with sugar
medronho	a schapps-like liqueur made from the fruit of the strawberry tree
vinho verde	young, slightly sparkling wine

small print & Index

SMALL PRINT

A Rough Guide to Rough Guides

Algarve DIRECTIONS is published by Rough Guides. The first *Rough Guide to Greece*, published in 1982, was a student scheme that became a publishing phenomenon. The immediate success of the book – with numerous reprints and a Thomas Cook prize shortlisting – spawned a series that rapidly covered dozens of destinations. Rough Guides had a ready market among low-budget backpackers, but soon also acquired a much broader and older readership that relished Rough Guides' wit and inquisitiveness as much as their enthusiastic, critical approach. Everyone wants value for money, but not at any price. Rough Guides soon began supplementing the "rougher" information about hostels and low-budget listings with the kind of detail on restaurants and quality hotels that independent-minded visitors on any budget might expect, whether on business in New York or trekking in Thailand. These days the guides offer recommendations from shoestring to luxury and cover a large number of destinations around the globe, including almost every country in the Americas and Europe, more than half of Africa and most of Asia and Australasia. Rough Guides now publish:

- Travel guides to more than 200 worldwide destinations
- Dictionary phrasebooks to 22 major languages
- Maps printed on rip-proof and waterproof Polyart™ paper
- Music guides running the gamut from Opera to Elvis
- Reference books on topics as diverse as the Weather and Shakespeare
- World Music CDs in association with World Music Network

Publishing information

This 1st edition published May 2005 by
Rough Guides Ltd, 80 Strand, London WC2R 0RL.
345 Hudson St, 4th Floor, New York, NY 10014, USA.

Distributed by the Penguin Group
Penguin Books Ltd, 80 Strand, London WC2R 0RL
Penguin Group (USA), 375 Hudson Street, NY 10014, USA
Penguin Group (Australia), 487 Maroondah Highway, PO Box 257, Ringwood, Victoria 3134, Australia
Penguin Group (Canada), 10 Alcorn Avenue, Toronto, Ontario, Canada M4V 1E4
Penguin Group (NZ), 182–190 Wairau Road, Auckland 10, New Zealand
Typeset in Bembo and Helvetica to an original design by Henry Iles.
Printed and bound in China by Leo

208pp includes index

A catalogue record for this book is available from the British Library

ISBN 1-84353-419-3

The publishers and authors have done their best to ensure the accuracy and currency of all the information in **Algarve DIRECTIONS**. However, they can accept no responsibility for any loss, injury, or inconvenience sustained by any traveller as a result of information or advice contained in the guide.

1 3 5 7 9 8 6 4 2

Help us update

We've gone to a lot of effort to ensure that the first edition of **Algarve DIRECTIONS** is accurate and up-to-date. However, things change – places get "discovered", opening hours are notoriously fickle, restaurants and rooms raise prices or lower standards. If you feel we've got it wrong or left something out, we'd like to know, and if you can remember the address, the price, the phone number, so much the better.

We'll credit all contributions, and send a copy of the next edition (or any other DIRECTIONS guide or Rough Guide if you prefer) for the best letters. Everyone who writes to us and isn't already a subscriber will receive a copy of our full-colour thrice-yearly newsletter. Please mark letters: "**Algarve DIRECTIONS Update**" and send to: Rough Guides, 80 Strand, London WC2R 0RL, or Rough Guides, 4th Floor, 345 Hudson St, New York, NY 10014. Or send an email to **mail@roughguides.com**

Have your questions answered and tell others about your trip at **www.roughguides.atinfopop.com**

Rough Guide credits

Text editor: Fran Sandham
Layout: Andy Hilliard
Photography: Eddie Gerald
Cartography: Miles Irving
Picture editor: Mark Thomas

Proofreader: Margaret Doyle
Production: Julia Bovis
Design: Henry Iles
Cover art direction: Chloe Roberts

The author

Matthew Hancock fell in love with Portugal while working in Lisbon and later returned to the country to complete a 775-mile long walk along the Spanish-Portuguese border. He is also author of *Lisbon Directions* and *Madeira Directions* and co-author of *The Rough Guide to Portugal*.

Acknowledgements

The author would like to thank everyone who helped, especially ICEP; Amanda Tomlin; Alex and Olivia for researching kids' stuff; Pedras d'el Rei; Vila Galé and the Tivoli group; and everyone at Rough Guides, especially Fran Sandham, Mark Thomas, Andy Hilliard and Miles Irving, and Margaret Doyle for proofreading.

Thanks also to the following for their especially helpful letters: Alan Bolister, Michael Freeman, Beryl and David Frost, Kathy Holroyd, Mats Kullstedt, Sara Mellen, Eva Noble, Gillian Oakes, Johnny Pring and Marian Smith.

Photo credits

All images © Rough Guides except the following:

p.1 Portuguese road sign in the Algarve © eye35.com/Alamy
p.10 Albufeira © Matthew Hancock
p.11 Silves © Matthew Hancock
p.22 Nave of San Lourenço Church © Hans Greg Roth/Corbis
p.24 Cork Trees at São Bras © John Miller
p.25 Mediterranean chameleon © Hans Dietan Brand/Corbis
p.27 Football match at the Faro Loulé Stadium © Michael Dalder/Corbis
p.30 Dolphin display at Zoo Marine © Malcolm Thornton/Alamy
p.35 Dolphin watching at Vilamoura © Matthew Hancock

p.35 Boat trip up the Guadiana © Matthew Hancock
p.36 Alte © Matthew Hancock
p.37 Alcoutim © Matthew Hancock
p.37 Salir © Matthew Hancock
p.38 Almond blossoms © Mark. E Gobson/Corbis
p.38 Festa de Santos Populares © John Van Hasselt/Corbis
p.38 Mae Soberana, Loulé © Cor Magnon/Alamy
p.39 Sardine Festival © Owen Franken/Corbis
p.39 Coral beer in glass © imagebroker/Alamy
p.48 Old windmill © Matthew Hancock
p.72 Salir © Matthew Hancock
p.103 Alcoutim © Matthew Hancock

Index

Map entries are marked in colour